KNOW YOUR HORSE

SUSAN McBANE

KNOW YOUR HORSE

How to *really* understand the way your horse
thinks and behaves

THUNDER BAY
P·R·E·S·S

San Diego, California

Thunder Bay Press
An imprint of the Advantage Publishers Group
10350 Barnes Canyon Road, San Diego, CA 92121
www.thunderbaybooks.com

Text, design, and photography © Octopus Publishing Group Ltd 2008

First published in Great Britain in 2008 by
Hamlyn, a division of Octopus Publishing Group Ltd
2–4 Heron Quays, London E14 4JP
www.octopusbooks.co.uk

Distributed in the United States and Canada by
Hachette Book Group USA,
237 Park Avenue, New York, NY 10017

Copyright under International, Pan American, and Universial
Copyright Conventions. All rights reserved. No part of this work may
be reproduced or transmitted in any form or by any means, electronic
or mechanical, including photocopying, recording or by any
information storage-and-retrieval system, without written permission
from the copyright holder. Brief passages (not to exceed 1,000 words)
may be quoted for reviews.

Printed and bound in China.
1 2 3 4 5 12 11 10 09 08

Library of Congress Cataloging-in-Publication Data

McBane, Susan.
Know your horse : how to really understand the way your horse thinks
and behaves / Susan McBane.
    p. cm.
Includes index.
ISBN-13: 978-1-59223-960-3
ISBN-10: 1-59223-960-9
1. Horses--Behavior. I. Title.
SF281.M332 2008
636.1--dc22

                                    2008029462

"Thunder Bay" is a registered trademark of Baker & Taylor. All rights
reserved.

All notations of errors or omissions should be sent to Thunder
Bay Press, Editorial Department, at the above address. All other
correspondence (author inquiries, permissions, and rights)
concerning the content of this book should be addressed to
Hamlyn, 2–4 Heron Quays, London E14 4JP, United Kingdom.

Note The advice in this book is provided as general information
only. It is not necessarily specific to any individual case and is
not a substitute for the guidance and advice provided by a
licensed veterinary practitioner consulted in any particular
situation. Neither Octopus Publishing Group nor the author
accepts any liability or responsibility for any consequences
resulting from the use of or reliance upon the information
contained herein. In this book, unless the information is given
specifically for female horses, horses are referred to as "he." The
information is equally applicable to both male and female
horses, unless otherwise specified. No horses or ponies were
harmed in the making of this book.

Contents

Introduction

Horse owners and riders are becoming more interested in equine behavior. An important topic in its own right, it is certainly a fascinating subject, not only because horses constantly do unexpected things and surprise us—just when we think we finally have them figured out. The reasons for this are the differences between the functioning of their brain and ours, and the fact that they are prey animals, and we are, essentially, predators. Our mind-sets are simply not the same.

Irrational behavior?

The inconvenient truth is that horses do not think in the same ways we do. Because of this, some people label them as stupid or irrational for reacting (or not reacting at all) in a way we would not expect to a given situation. A horse might spook at a harmless plastic bag lying at the side of the road, yet ignore the biggest, noisiest truck thundering past. Many a horse has been given a sound whipping because he behaved in a way that was natural and appropriate for him, but not what his human companion either wanted or expected.

Using this book

The aim of this book is to try to explain many puzzling aspects of horse behavior: why things happen as they do, and what, if anything, can or should be done about them. Not all horse behaviors are wrong.

Special feature sections provide information that is important to understanding horse psychology and behavior. A general overview is often necessary to get a full picture before dealing with specific aspects or problems. By the end of the book, you should have an accurate view and clearer understanding of equine behavior and psychology.

They're all different

Like humans and other animals, horses are individuals with different characters and personalities, but there are nevertheless some basic factors that apply to them all.

It is also widely believed that there are marked differences in character and temperament between breeds—but things are not always as they seem. So-called hot-blooded breeds—which include thoroughbreds, Arabians, and mixed breeds with a high proportion of this breeding in them—are often regarded as reactive, oversensitive, difficult, and not for novices. Generally this is true, but there are many such animals that are sensible, kind, able to judge a person's abilities and character, and act accordingly. Other equine types traditionally regarded as placid, safe, and quiet—such as cobs, native-type ponies, and horses with a good deal of cold or heavy-horse blood in them—can sometimes turn out to be edgy, high-strung, and far from quiet.

When learning about horse psychology and behavior, and in order to be safe and effective in your interactions with horses, it is essential to be able to judge each horse as an individual while working within general guidelines applicable to all horses.

I hope and believe that this book will offer an accurate—and sometimes unique—view of equine psychology and will help you get into the mind of your horse. I also hope that the knowledge you gain will encourage and enable you to cultivate the important qualities of quietness, patience, and understanding in handling, riding, and caring for your horse. This does not mean displaying weakness and submission to what is a potentially dangerous animal due to his size, strength, and lightning-fast reactions. Calmness with confidence, firmness with tact, and a positive attitude with the honesty to see things as they really are—not just as you would like them to be—are your keys to success with these (perhaps unexpectedly) sensitive animals.

Right: Horses are much more sensitive and emotional than many of us realize. Spending time getting up close and personal is worth the while.

UNDERSTAND YOUR HORSE

Before you can understand horses, you have to know what type of animal you are dealing with:

- Horses are prey animals. This gives them lightning-fast reactions to anything they perceive as startling or dangerous.
- They evolved as grazing animals that defend themselves by running away.
- Their senses—in particular, their eyesight— give them a different perception of the world than ours, which often accounts for their unexpected behavior.
- They are sociable herd animals that feel safer in friendly company, preferably of their own species.
- They learn both good and bad habits very quickly.

Horses are not complex animals, but need to be treated logically on the basis of a thorough understanding of their nature.

Horse basics

Let's look at five basic elements that shape a horse's behavior and consider what each one means for the horse-human relationship. This will provide a brief summary of the basic points on each topic.

What is instinctive behavior?

This is behavior that horses display naturally in response to given situations—behavior they are hardwired to perform and which they cannot help doing. Horses can be trained to modify their reactions, but if pushed too far into a situation they find frightening or confusing, they will revert to their instinctive behavior of fleeing if they can, or fighting if cornered: the famous fight-or-flight response.

Prey animals

Although horses do not live on edge all the time, they need to keep watch on their surroundings in order to check for predators and often prefer a location with an all-around view to satisfy this instinct. An unfamiliar noise or sudden movement are prime causes of a horse becoming startled and switching immediately into panic mode, since these things indicate to him that a predator could be nearby.

A change in the environment can create suspicion and cause a horse to become unsure and defensive. For example, if a horse is used to being in a particular area and suddenly an unfamiliar object or person appears—or even a familiar person who this time happens to be carrying an open umbrella, for example—he could become unsure or even frightened. We may know it is quite safe, but the horse does not and might shy or stop dead in his tracks.

Grazing, running animals

Horses need plenty of fibrous food such as grass, hay, or haylage. They do not thrive if kept short of fiber and may suffer digestive problems such as colic and stomach ulcers. Hardworking domestic horses should be fed at least two-thirds of their diet as high-energy fiber, and those working lightly to moderately do well on a diet that is all or mostly medium- or low-energy fiber.

Running is one of the things horses do best. Creatures originally of wide-open grassy plains, horses like space and are most comfortable when they feel they have room to run away should danger present itself. They can adapt to enclosed spaces such as stables if they associate them with comfort and safety, although freedom is important to their mental and physical health.

Equine senses

Horses' eyesight is very different than ours, so if a horse spooks (shies), refuses to go somewhere, or insists on moving his head around (which he needs to do in order to focus), make allowances for this. Their hearing is very acute and they are able to hear higher-pitched sounds than we can, which may account for distracted behavior. Horses' sense of smell is far more powerful than ours and is important to them for identifying food, people, and other animals, including those who have recently passed by. (For more on equine senses, see pages 12–13.) Their natural suspiciousness makes their sense of taste very important when choosing food.

Herd animals

Horses evolved over millions of years as sociable herd animals and their instinct to be with other equines is extremely strong. There is safety in numbers and most horses feel insecure when alone. They prefer at least one other horse or pony for company; failing that, some do form friendships with other species, but this is a poor alternative.

Fast learners

Successful prey animals need to learn quickly, and horses do so. Making the same mistake twice can end their life. In domestication, horses have to learn about being ridden or driven, surviving in a stable yard or fenced field, coping with humans and other animals, and how the outside world operates. Unfortunately, they learn things we do not want them to do just as quickly as those we want them to. Everything we do with horses teaches them something—and horses have excellent memories. When schooling horses, therefore, we must be careful to use correct methods and reward them the instant they get it right, otherwise they can become confused.

The horse's senses

Horses have the same senses we do, but they operate rather differently. A horse's perception of the world is therefore not like ours and this can result in behavior we find difficult to interpret and understand.

Above: Horses first use their eyes and ears, then will smell and maybe taste something interesting. It seems that cats do the same thing!

Vision

Horses can see almost all around them. Their eyes are set high on their head and to the sides, so they see mainly separate views with each eye (monocular vision) and only see with both eyes (binocular vision) directly in front of them. However, here there is a blind spot for a distance of about six feet.

Horses see in a narrow streak (known as the visual streak) of fairly sharp vision, with areas above and below being more blurred. The muscles controlling the lens in the eye are not strong, so a horse cannot focus easily by altering the shape of the lens, as we do. Instead, he will move his head into various positions to bring what he wants to look at on to the visual streak. This means that if a ridden horse's head is overly restricted, he may struggle to free his head from restraint so that he can see properly.

Because horses have almost 360-degree vision and need to make only small movements of the head to take in the blind areas, they easily spot things we do not notice and may become startled by them, perhaps leaping about or swinging around to see them more clearly.

Horses are not color-blind, although they probably perceive colors in a manner akin to color-blind humans. They also probably see best in dim light rather than in bright light or darkness, and naturally tend to be more active around dawn and dusk.

Smell

The equine sense of smell is almost as good as that of canines. Horses can detect smells produced by other creatures, substances, objects, and growing things, including scents on the ground and in the air.

All horses have a special structure, the Jacobson's organ, high up in the nose. They will sniff in a smell, raise their head and upper lip, and close the nostrils so that they can assess the scent with this organ. This action is called flehmen; when a horse does it, he is not laughing, as is sometimes thought.

Taste

The taste buds on the horse's tongue can detect sweet, salty, sour, and bitter tastes. A horse will test an unfamiliar substance by smelling it, then he might try tasting it. Like humans, horses can develop a taste for unhealthy things such as poisonous plants, but most are normally fastidious feeders, which is why they often will not eat feed with medicine in it.

Hearing

Horses have acute hearing and can also hear higher-pitched sounds than we can. Each of the outer ears can move around 180 degrees, independently, so sounds can be gathered from all around. Because horses pick up sounds we cannot hear, they may react to them by becoming distracted or jumpy.

The ears tell us where the horse is directing his attention and also indicate his mood. If they are turned forward, the horse is intrigued by something ahead; if they flop to the sides, he is relaxed, sleepy, or unwell; if they are pressed flat back on his neck, he is angry or concentrating very hard on something.

Touch

Horses have hypersensitive skin, despite its being covered with hair. It is easily irritated by things such as a fly landing on it; dried-up dirt or bits of bedding being rubbed in by rugs or tack (saddle or bridle), rough grooming, tickly touches, and, of course, abuse from whips, spurs, and bits. However, horses usually love a comforting rubdown or massage given by someone confident and caring, with a good sense of touch not so hard that it is unpleasant nor so light that it irritates and tickles.

Above: *This horse is paying attention to the photographer (his left ear is pointed toward the camera) and to something off to his right at the same time (his right ear is sideways)—good survival instincts.*

Normal temperament

Like all humans and other creatures, horses have individual temperaments that can vary. However, there are certain general qualities they possess as a species. Understanding the species and knowing your horse as an individual will help you understand his sometimes quirky behavior.

Above: Horses always feel calm and secure in the company of other horses they know and like, unless something stressful is happening. They can grow to feel this way about humans, too.

What is it?

Horses by nature are not aggressive. They are not hunters that kill to eat or have a den to protect, and are not generally regarded as territorial with an area to defend, although they do try to own an area when they are in it, and the herd stallion will mark its boundaries with his dung (see pages 34–35). Because of these factors, horses can be regarded as normally peace-loving, sociable animals when they are among their familiar companions, equine or otherwise.

Triggers for change

If your horse's normal temperament changes, find out if something is bothering him (see box). A contented horse behaves normally for him as an individual, so only situations that worry or irritate him will trigger a change. Remember that, like people or other animals, not all horses are naturally sweet-natured.

What to do

Look through the topics in the box and consider whether any of them could apply to your horse. If you are not sure, ask a caring, knowledgeable person to help.

A change in temperament could have a physical cause, such as illness or pain. If you suspect this may be the case, a checkup by your vet could reveal something about which you had no idea. If there is no physical cause, your vet might have some suggestions about your horse's management and lifestyle.

Other experts, such as a sympathetic teacher, physical therapist, or behavioral practitioner, could help you put things right.

ASK YOURSELF

Does your horse appear off-color or ill?

Is he standing at the back of his stable or away from other horses in the field, looking listless? Is he lying down more or less than usual? Is he eating and drinking normally? Are his temperature, pulse, and respiration normal (see pages 48–49)? Is he lame, and/or does he have any sores, wounds, swellings, or lumps on his body or legs?

▷ *Any of these signs can indicate a physical problem and you should consult your vet.*

Does your horse appear irritated, anxious, or frightened, and/or is he more restless than usual?

This can happen when a new horse comes into a yard or is introduced into the field, or your horse feels threatened by or dislikes a particular horse. It can also happen when your horse's friend has been taken away or he is left alone, which worries many horses.

▷ *Try your best to ensure that your horse lives with animals he likes and is not stabled near or turned out with those he does not get along with.*

Does your horse's behavior change only when you (or another person) are around?

This can mean he does not trust you (or that person), or is worried by what you (or they) are doing with him, whether it involves riding, shoeing, grooming, or anything else.

▷ *Strengthen your relationship with him by means of quiet, strong, caring handling and riding. Horses are sensitive and need gentle, confident handling, and a rider with a firm, protective leadership attitude. If someone else is causing your horse to feel unsettled, you should politely but firmly ask what they are doing, explain why they need to stop, and ask them to do so. If they do not, you need to make sure they no longer handle your horse, or move your horse to another yard.*

Above left: *Relaxing with your horse will help keep him calm, but remember that horses can react to disturbing stimuli in their surroundings, so be aware of this and ensure your personal safety at all times.*

Herd instincts

Horses are strongly gregarious, and this can cause problems when working with and caring for them. There is a lot of misunderstanding over how herds function, so watching feral or domestic herds with an open mind can teach you a lot.

What are they?

Herd instincts are those that keep the herd together and work for its survival, and domestic horses still function along these lines. Because of this, animals leaving the herd—in feral herds, males being rejected by the resident stallion or others wanting to join it—can upset the remaining herd members. Those leaving to form new herds will take time to establish their relationships. However, in time things will settle down, as horses are very adaptable.

Another powerful herd instinct is the drive to find food and water, and to graze together. In a given region, an experienced herd member—usually an older female—knows where the water and best grazing are at particular times, so the herd will naturally want to follow her.

The stallion's role

A stallion's instinct is to keep his herd for himself, rounding up its members closely if a competitor appears and fighting the interloper if he does not accept his warning signals to go away. However, he is not the herd leader as far as daily routine is concerned, but more of a protective lodger with breeding rights for a few years. The nucleus of the herd is the females.

Fight or flight

Horses are classic prey and flight animals. Their evolutionary environment favored animals that could run fast for their lives, as far as necessary. Horses' vision is geared more toward detecting movement than sharp detail, so it became instinctive to startle at any slight movement nearby and flee without investigating first.

Domestic horses still have this strong instinct and often gallop around a field together if one has reacted to an unfamiliar movement. Unfortunately, they can also do this when ridden, which is highly dangerous. One of the main aims of training is to suppress this instinct whenever humans are in charge.

Horses are not as stupid as some people make out. Feral equines know whether a predator such as a mountain lion or a wolf is on the hunt or just passing through, and will not flee merely at the sight of it. Domestic horses, too, judge situations

HOW TO USE THE HERD INSTINCT

- During training, use your horse's need for company and his tendency to follow the lead of other horses, particularly older, more experienced ones. Gradually you, the trainer, can take over—a "made," or schooled, horse does what his rider asks, as long as it is reasonable and possible.

- Turning horses out to field and bringing them in as a group can be problematic, but if you let a respected herd member such as an older mare (and her friend) lead the way, the others will often slot in quietly behind.

- In caring for your horse, you need to satisfy his instinct to eat fiber for most of the time. He is not being greedy: he is programmed to do this and will suffer psychological and physical distress if not allowed to do so.

- You also need to use and respect the herd instinct by providing a congenial herd environment for your horse, even if this is just one other friendly horse or pony, although most horses love being in a small herd of up to a dozen members. This natural way of life makes for horses that feel secure, safe, and settled.

and if they are confident in their surroundings will not take to their heels at every little disturbance. However, people who are overly excited around horses, people who run around and shout, can hype up horses easily. Depending on their individual temperaments, horses can then become worried, frightened, defensive (ready to use teeth and heels), or even aggressive. Good horse people remain calm and confident.

Above: The horse on the right is using typical stallion herding behavior—head down, with a snaking movement—to drive others (here a mare and her foal) to where he wants them to go.

Right: These mares, foals, and youngsters on the move are concerned about something. The horse on the left is clearly worried; take note of the foals' expressions: heads up and ears back.

Learning capacity

Horses learn quickly and have excellent memories. This can cause problems, as they learn from every situation in their lives, not just from their trainer during schooling sessions.

What is it?

Learning capacity is the horse's ability to learn, along with how much he is able to absorb. This latter appears to be much more than was previously believed. Horses not only learn quite quickly what the signals from a rider or driver mean (if they are taught correctly), but can also associate sounds such as verbal cues with objects or movements, or pick out colored cards from an array presented to them, for example. They also learn to associate certain sounds with particular situations, such as the rattle of buckets at feeding times or the sound of a particular vehicle with the arrival of his owner—and these are just a few examples.

Innate skills

Horses are prey animals, so they instinctively keep a close eye on their surroundings. This means that horses have become extremely perceptive of the smallest movements, signs, and changes in their environment. They are quick thinkers and to many people seem to be far more intelligent than is suggested by the small size of their brains in relation to their bodies.

Horses learn quickly by means of the association of ideas and formation of habits. They learn what aids and signals mean if these are taught in a calm manner using a logical, structured system, so that responding becomes a habit. Equine hearing is acute (see pages 12–13), so raising your voice is not only unnecessary but also counterproductive, as it can frighten them. A tense, nervous horse learns nothing except that he is probably in danger, and then his survival instincts kick in so that he will either fight or flee—neither of which is conducive to learning.

Can horses reason?

The accepted view among most scientifically trained people such as zoologists, vets, and behaviorists is that horses cannot reason. This is because horses lack an enlarged right neocortex and prefrontal cortex in the brain, the parts responsible for higher mental functions like reasoning, which are present only in humans, the great apes, dolphins, and whales.

Some scientists and many lay horse people believe that horses are capable of reasoning and claim to have proved it through

experiments. Others argue that all that has happened is that the horses in these instances have learned to respond correctly, maybe initially by trial and error, and associated the act with a reward of some kind, so that the response subsequently became habitual.

In practice

Probably the most important thing to remember is that horses have a limited concentration span. They seem to be able to concentrate intensively for only a few minutes, probably no more than five at most. After this, they start directing their attention to something else. If under saddle, they may well continue doing whatever their rider is asking, but are clearly not really concentrating. After a short rest, however, they will start attending to their rider again.

This demonstrates that it is not good schooling practice to drill horses for long periods—say, thirty to forty minutes, or even longer—as is so often the case. Even humans can only concentrate fully for around twenty-five minutes at a time, so it is unreasonable to expect more from a horse.

Above: If taught in a calm and logical manner, horses have a great capacity to learn habitual responses to verbal, physical, and aural aids.

Left: Long-reining helps develop a horse's confidence and trust, which makes for more effective learning.

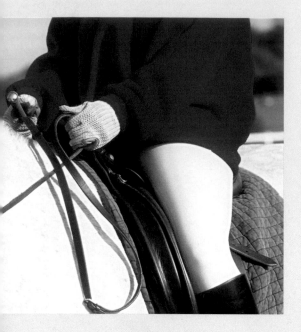

Humans have trained horses for thousands of years. Very often, even today, this has involved the use of force and draconian methods by the less intelligent and caring. Others do care for their animals but treat them as having similar mental abilities to humans, which horses don't possess. Burdening horses with such inappropriate expectations, even unwittingly, can distress them and produce unsatisfactory results for the trainer, and also spoil the horses.

Learning theory

WHAT IS IT?

Learning theory is the scientific approach to training animals according to the way in which they behave in the environment for which they evolved. It also takes into account how a species's biology affects its behavior; you would not expect a horse to behave like a bird, for example.

LEARNING: DEFINITIONS

Learning is something we all understand but may find difficult to put into words, so here are three definitions. Learning is:

A relatively permanent change in the probability of the occurrence of a response due to experience. As a result of training, the horse responds reliably to an aid (rider's signal), whereas previously he did not.

Remembering associations. For example, the rider squeezes with both legs, the horse moves forward, and the rider immediately stops squeezing. The horse learns to associate moving forward with the subsequent cessation of the aid, so if he wants the rider to stop squeezing (which is more comfortable for the horse) he now knows that moving forward produces this result—at least if the aid is applied by a rider using logical training methods.

Any process in an animal in which its behavior becomes consistently modified as a result of experience. The horse learns to consistently modify (reliably change) his behavior when he feels the aid or hears the command. A leg squeeze means to move forward and results in the squeeze stopping, and in time this becomes an ingrained habit—if the aid is consistently applied and, most importantly, consistently stopped the instant the horse gives the desired response.

LOGICAL SCHOOLING TECHNIQUES

Horse training appears to have a long way to go before it can be regarded as a scientifically founded process. Although logical, scientifically proven methods are widely used with other animals, the traditional horse world does not appear to be interested. Whole books have been written on the subject, but here are two examples of techniques that work well—because they are in accord with how the horse's brain works—but which most horse trainers do not adopt:

Hands without legs, legs without hands. This means that the rider must not use the hand and leg aids at precisely the same moment. In simple terms, young horses are taught that a pull on the reins means to slow down or stop, and a squeeze from the legs

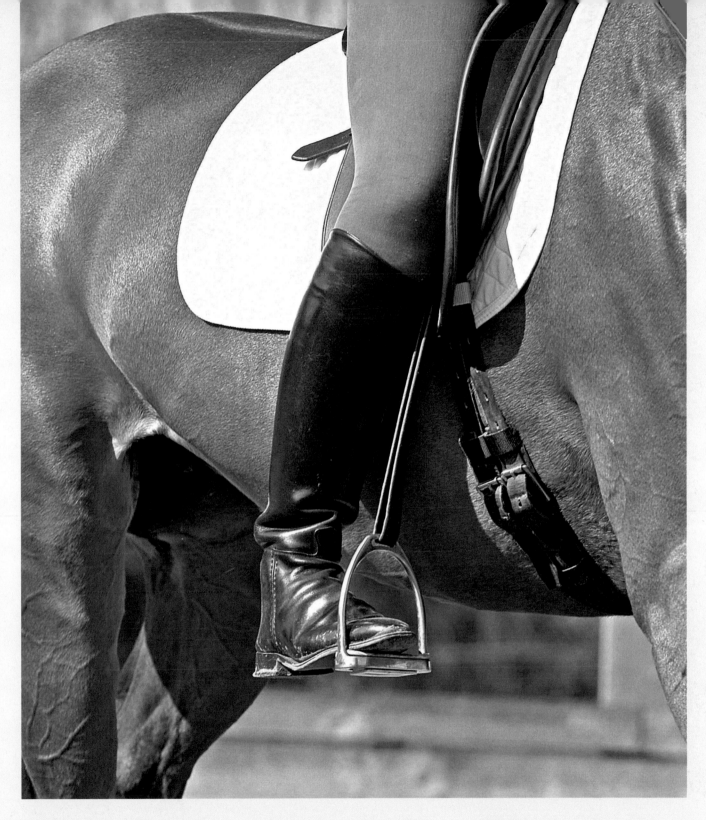

means to go forward. Therefore, if the hand and leg aids are applied at the same time, they constitute contradictory requests, which confuses the horse.

Train the horse to go in self-balance. This can be done from the earliest days of training, rather than supporting him by letting him lean on the bit, or encouraging him to do so in the mistaken belief that this will help him to accept the bit. Horses go much more lightly, comfortably, confidently, and willingly when taught to balance themselves.

Far left: This rider is holding the reins correctly, with the rein under the ring finger, which is the weakest and most sensitive finger.

Above: A good leg position, behind the girth to guide the horse's hindquarters and legs. (This girth is well back from the elbow, so will not restrict the horse's action.)

Mental needs

The mental needs of horses are no different from those of other animals and humans: basically, they want to feel comfortable and safe. This doesn't seem much to ask, but many of the things we do with and to horses actually have the opposite effect. We need to remember that when horses are unhappy or worried, their survival instincts soon come into play. They become difficult and even dangerous to handle—whereas when they feel confident and secure, they are much safer and a pleasure to deal with.

Fulfilling your horse's needs

Although horses have been domesticated for about 6,000 years, they still retain their wild instincts, and their minds and bodies still function like those of wild animals, especially when things go wrong. If owners want to keep their horses happy, contented, and healthy in domestic conditions, they would be advised to follow this simple but comprehensive plan. Professionals in the field of animal management devised the "Five Freedoms" for the care of all animals, including horses. The freedoms relate to every aspect of a horse's life, including care, management, riding, and schooling.

1. Freedom from thirst, hunger, and malnutrition. Whether stabled or turned out, your horse should have fresh food and, most importantly, clean water available nearly all the time. His diet should be devised—perhaps with the aid of your vet—to provide enough energy and nutrients for his work and to maintain good health, without him becoming either fat or thin.

2. Freedom from physical and thermal discomfort. Horses are sensitive and overheat easily. Stables and shelters should protect them from bad winter weather, wind, and rain, but also from hot sun and flies. Ideally, horses should be able to come and go as they wish. Housing should be large enough to allow a horse to get down, roll, sleep flat out, and get up again with confidence, with a thick, dry bed and good ventilation. A paddock needs a safe, flat area where the horses can lie down and rest.

3. Freedom from pain, injury, and disease. You should handle and ride your horse in ways that do not cause him pain or put him at risk of injury. His vaccinations and worming program must be up to date, and his feet and teeth should be kept in good hygiene. You also need the knowledge to realize when your horse requires first aid or veterinary attention for an injury or suspected disease.

4. Freedom to express most patterns of normal behavior. Horses are herd animals: most will not thrive or be fully content without regular, social contact with their own kind. You need to allow your horse the liberty and company necessary to fulfill his equine behavior patterns on a daily basis, more or less. This behavior includes rolling, mutual grooming, and running and playing with others in a safely fenced area.

5. Freedom from fear and distress. Handling and working horses in ways that produce discomfort or pain can cause them mental suffering. These include using badly fitted or adjusted tack and clothing, harsh bits and harsh riding and schooling techniques, inhumane use of whips and spurs, demanding that the horse accomplish tasks that are too difficult, or working him too hard or for too long. Horses need to feel safe with their attendants, not frightened of them. Mental suffering can also result from keeping horses without companions, in boring environments, and with insufficient water and fibrous food.

Left: Stabling youngsters together in a big stable is reassuring for them, especially when the door is a comfortable height for them to get their heads over easily and see what is going on outside.

Above: Horses can drink from quite shallow water, as shown by this shire horse drinking from a puddle. There are also horses who like to dunk their whole muzzle.

READING YOUR HORSE

One-way conversations are rarely
productive and always leave one party
feeling frustrated. In the equestrian
world, that party is usually the horse.
If you stand quietly and watch horses
together, ideally where they can behave
naturally, you will find that they do not
make much noise. They do have voices,
of course, and will use them, but their
main means of communication is through
body language. This chapter explains
how to interpret what your horse is
saying, to you or others.

Body language

Horses are extremely perceptive animals and notice tiny changes in their surroundings that would probably escape our attention. This includes the body postures, attitudes, and positions of other creatures—equine, human, and otherwise.

What is it?

Body language is the horse's primary way of interpreting what others are communicating and how they are feeling. By watching body attitudes and signals, and using them himself, a horse can understand clearly the feelings of other creatures and communicate his own to them. Horses are constantly well informed about the mood of the moment.

Let's consider some common body attitudes of horses in different emotional states.

Relaxed greeting

Whether he is stabled or free, as you approach your horse, his ears will prick forward toward you and he will raise his head and look at you with both eyes, although he may have previously noticed you with just one. His nostrils will probably flare open a little to smell you—just to make sure it's you—as he walks toward you. His tail will be relaxed and swinging, neither particularly raised nor clamped down. As he relaxes in your presence, he will probably resume eating, his eyes will remain soft, and his ears will relax to the sides.

Alert

If a horse sees something that takes his attention, he will raise his head quickly and look directly at it, his ears pricked forward toward it and both eyes wide open looking at it. His tail may be raised a little, and he will probably stand foursquare and absolutely still while he stares and assesses the object or creature. He may then decide to approach it or move away, either slowly or quickly.

Alarmed

In this state, a horse is often on the verge of following his natural instincts and running away. His body will be tense and the muscles hard, and he may be trembling. His head and tail will be up and his ears and eyes directed toward whatever is causing him concern. He will usually want to face it to keep it in view, but may soon wheel away on his hind legs and gallop off.

Sleepy

A horse can doze and sleep lightly while standing up so that he can run away quickly should danger approach. His head will be about level with his withers, his ears flopping to the sides and his eyes half-closed. His tail will be low and

relaxed, and he may well be resting a hind leg on the toe of the hoof, with his hip dropped.

Sick or exhausted

Novice owners often confuse a sleepy horse with a sick or tired one, but with practice you will learn to tell the difference. A sick horse will stay away from others and will stand like a sleepy horse but often without resting a hind leg (he may also lie down more than usual). His head may be low and he may have other symptoms such as trembling or sweating, and perhaps an anxious or distressed look on his face. If your horse is displaying these symptoms, seek veterinary help immediately.

Above: This gray horse looks suspicious and worried, as shown by his ears pointed forward, his wide eyes, flared (open) nostrils, and tense head and neck.

Right: Making good use of his survival instinct to flee from danger, this horse is galloping away to his right while still keeping his left eye on whatever is bothering him.

Although we are vertical animals and horses horizontal, the similarities between our own body language and theirs is remarkable. No matter what shape an animal is, others usually reliably recognize what its body language conveys, from emotions to messages and intentions. Most horses are not aggressive, and treating them as though they are through failing to recognize a submissive or friendly demeanor can cause major problems.

Submissive body language

WHICH HORSES ARE SUBMISSIVE?

Young horses are usually submissive to their elders. Although they may not begin that way, most mature equines will put a youngster in his place if he misbehaves. A mare will usually shield her very young foal (up to a few weeks old) from other herd members, but he

RIDDEN SUBMISSION

One of the difficulties with riding your horse as opposed to observing him from the ground is that you cannot see his body language or facial expression. However, you can still pick up on his state of mind. A horse that is happy to go along with what you want is calm and relaxed (stroke his neck to feel the tone of the muscles) and responds easily to your aids—you could call him submissive. One that is frightened, angry, or objecting may thrash his tail (which you can feel and hear), clamp his ears back, chomp noticeably on the bit, and have hard, tense muscles.

will gradually be allowed more freedom. Once he starts exploring—and approaching or accepting approaches from other herd members, including foals and older horses—he builds on the equine body language he has learned from his dam. Instinct plays a part, but he will pick up some actions, postures, and facial expressions from others.

Older horses are sometimes submissive. Signs of submission from one horse to a more dominant one can include simply keeping away or moving away from him; moving on when he approaches; giving way over resources such as grazing, companions, or shelter; and not defending himself when harassed.

Youngsters and horses with an unconfident nature sometimes make signs of submission to humans—youngsters may even make such signs to dogs.

Left: This foal is performing a classic "don't hurt me" action, snapping his front teeth together rapidly, with his head and neck outstretched and lowered.

Right: The stallion on the left is showing interest in the mare on the right by pricking his ears toward her—but hers are back, indicating that she is not so enthusiastic.

WHAT TO LOOK FOR

The body positions and actions a horse makes when he wishes to convey submission, acceptance, or an easygoing nature are:

- Expression in the eyes is soft and inquiring.
- Head is held level with the withers, or lower.
- Ears are softly forward or a little to the side.
- Muzzle and nostrils are soft and relaxed.
- Tail is held normally, or a little low.

This posture is mainly seen in more submissive horses, and not necessarily only in youngsters. The clearest sign of submission is that the horse will snap his front teeth together, his lower jaw moving up and down a few times in a motion called snapping. This has nothing to do with nipping, snapping in aggression, or biting.

OTHER SUBMISSIVE ACTS

A submissive horse will be quick to move away from one with a stronger or more dominant personality. If a skirmish breaks out, he will keep out of trouble and give it a wide berth. A horse with a stronger personality that the others respect does not have to make his presence or wishes known. Others back away, give him room, and do not hassle him.

IN THE HERD

In a natural herd, there is very little argument or what we see as pushing for position. The population is relatively stable and there is little reason for arguments. It is in domestic herds—and most especially those on establishments with floating populations such as livery yards—that behavior changes most and you have the chance to observe it.

The sounds horses make

Horses do not use their voices much, but they do have a useful range of sounds. In addition to those they make with their voice boxes, they produce other noises, such as snorts and grunts, all of which have a meaning that we can learn to interpret.

Below: Whinnying horses can sometimes look as if they are laughing. They usually raise their heads to create free airflow through the larynx, flare their nostrils, and open their mouths a little.

Right: There will be a good deal of squealing going on in this altercation. These ponies, though, do not look at all aggressive and are simply indulging in classic horseplay.

Vocal sounds

Neigh The best-known horse sound, this is a loud, vibrating noise, almost reaching a scream in an angry stallion. It can be ear-piercing if you are standing next to the horse. If you are riding him, you will feel his whole body shake and vibrate underneath you. The neigh denotes a mating call between mare and stallion, a call for attention and greeting, or a call to a horse or other creature (including a person) that is some way off. It can indicate pleasure and surprise, but also anxiety and insecurity, such as when a horse calls for others when he is in a strange place or alone.

Whinny This is a scaled-down version of the neigh that is softer and deeper, denoting expectation and pleasure, maybe at seeing a person or animal the horse associates with good experiences. It is used for people or other animals that are fairly near to the horse.

Nicker or whicker Further down the volume scale, this is an intimate, soft, deep, vibrating sound that denotes pleasure, welcome, and anticipation. It is usually directed toward a person or horse standing close by, when the two are reunited following a separation. For example, when a horse is taken out for work and later returns, the friend he left behind will welcome him home with a neigh or whinny, which soon descends to a nicker as the two make contact again.

Squealing A squeal is a short, high-pitched sound that horses make when they are playing but also when there is an argument. They also sometimes squeal when experiencing a sudden pain. A squeal can indicate annoyance and may be accompanied by a nip.

Groan When in pain, a horse will produce a long, low moan that is terrible to hear. His eyes might look sunken and his ears will be sideways or back.

Nonvocal sounds

Grunt Horses often grunt when making a major physical effort, such as when getting up, jumping a large fence, or performing a difficult movement. They often grunt after a bowel movement as well.

Snort When a horse blows air hard through his flared nostrils, this denotes excitement. Horses do this when near something that is exciting and perhaps a little worrying, or if they are expecting trouble from another horse.

High blowing This noise often worries novice owners. However, it does not indicate a respiratory problem but is caused by the false nostril (a flap of skin inside each nostril) vibrating when the horse has his breathing restricted—for example, if the rider pulls in his head, cramping his throat area—forcing the horse to try hard to get air in and out.

Roaring and whistling These are two noises made when a horse with a defective larynx or voice box breathes in. Roaring is a deeper sound than whistling. A nerve malfunction prevents one or both vocal cords from being drawn back during inhalation and the noise is made by the air rushing past them. Because this disorder reduces the airflow through the larynx, the horse cannot breathe well enough to be worked at paces such as a fast canter or gallop. Surgery is the only solution, but then the horse usually cannot use his voice at all.

The horse's emotions

It is amazing how many people, even those who are experienced, think that horses do not feel emotions in significant measure. This is quite wrong; horses are not only sensitive but emotional too.

Recognizing equine emotions

We can tell how horses are feeling from their body language (see pages 26–29) and behavior. Individual body parts (mainly the ears, eyes, muzzle, tail, and legs) are held and positioned in certain ways, but an overall picture that includes all these signs is the most helpful.

An experienced person can tell instantly just by looking at a horse how he is feeling. This may be due partly to that person's innate sensitivity, but it also comes with experience if you remain open to the feelings coming from the horse. This may sound a little far-fetched, but in time any reasonably caring person will begin to sense such things.

The main emotions horses experience can be divided into groups of related feelings. The late Dr. Moyra Williams, a clinical psychologist and horse breeder, placed them in four groups:

1. Pain, fear, and anxiety
2. Apprehension and anger
3. Anticipation, peace, happiness, and enjoyment
4. Excitement, exhaustion, and submission

Some signs—such as relaxation, skin tension, ear position, tail posture, and others—apply to a variety of emotions, so the following are a few general pointers to help you interpret what your horse is feeling.

Ears, eyes, and muzzle

The facial expressions and the general look of the head are very informative. The eyes can look bright and interested or sunken and sad. The tension of the skin tells us whether the horse is upset or calm, and the ears too, either tense or softer. These body parts tell us most about a horse's feelings. For example:

- A **happy** horse's ears will be held sideways or loosely forward, with his head up a little. His eyes may be half-closed and his muzzle will be relaxed.
- A **frightened** horse's ears will be back, his head up, and his eyes wide open, looking at what is frightening him. His muzzle will be stiff and tense, and will probably display flared nostrils.

- An **angry** horse's head will point outward (unless his handler prevents this) and his ears will be pressed flat back. His eyes will be wide open—maybe showing the whites—and looking at his problem, and he may show his teeth.
- A **submissive** horse's ears will point backward or to the sides, his head will point outward (unless his handler prevents this), and his eyes may be half-closed. His lips (and maybe jaw) will make a characteristic snapping movement, opening and closing fairly rapidly (see pages 28–29).

Tail

The horse's tail is also a good guide to his feelings. Linking it to the examples above:

Happiness: Tail loose
Fear: Tail flat or clamped between buttocks
Anger: Tail "whisking" (thrashing about)
Submission: Tail flat and limp

Other signs

Your horse's general attitude and the feeling you get from him are good indicators of his emotions. If his body is relaxed he is feeling happy, peaceful, or any other positive emotion. If he looks tense, he is experiencing pain, fear, anxiety, apprehension, or excitement.

If you can get close enough in safety (beware if he is frightened or angry), your horse's skin and muscle tension will tell you a lot. They will feel loose in positive emotions and tight in negative ones.

Actual trembling is a clear sign of extreme, negative emotions such as fear, pain, anger, or anxiety—but make sure your horse is not simply shivering from cold before making your judgment.

You can tell a lot about your horse's usual mental state from his body condition. If he has a rather dull coat, he is probably not too healthy and is feeling under the weather. If he loses weight easily—particularly if he has a good deal of thoroughbred or Arab blood—this can mean that his life in general makes him anxious.

Left: This horse is rather anxious about something to his left, but also because he is being held by his handler and cannot get away from the problem. Note his pricked ears and tense muzzle.

Below: Horses and ponies kept alone often become sad and depressed, even though in natural conditions they can also develop abnormal behavior patterns and become more susceptible to illness.

How horses communicate

Horses communicate all the time, not just with each other but also with animals of other species and with humans. The big advantage for anyone trying to understand what they are saying is that they use the same language—or set of signs—no matter what species of creature they are trying to communicate with. The interesting thing is that other animals understand them far better than we do.

WHY IS THIS?

This is because humans primarily communicate vocally while animals make much more use of body language, including body attitudes or simple facial expressions. We, too, use body language (sometimes unwittingly) and facial expressions, but we are the only animals who use words to convey ideas and messages to each other.

OTHER WAYS OF COMMUNICATING

A major means of communication among animals, including horses, is smell: just about every animal has a better sense of smell than we do (see pages 12–13).

Stallions are well known for passing on an "I'm here, this is my territory" message through their droppings and urine. They seem to do it purposely by defecating on top of any rival male's droppings or, especially, on an invisible boundary dividing their herd's territory from that of a neighboring herd.

Stallions also often urinate on top of the droppings of other males (probably to mask their smell and replace it with their own scent) and of females (telling rivals that this female is spoken for). Free-living ones do their droppings around the boundaries of the area that they consider as belonging to their herd.

SOUNDS

As well as vocal sounds (see pages 30–31), horses use other sounds, usually to attract attention or release strong emotions. A common example is the horse that constantly bangs his stable door with his front feet. The solution always is to find out why he is banging (usually he needs to be turned out more with friends). If he still bangs, padding the door may reduce the incidents and protect his feet and legs. For more on door banging, see pages 80–81.

THOUGHT PICTURES

Some people take the view that horses communicate through thoughts and pictures, and then try this method with us but ultimately give up because we are clearly not tuned in to them.

A horse and rider that have a very close bond with each other do seem to be able to communicate by means of thoughts. The rider imagines them and their horse performing a specific movement or in a particular way and combines this with the normal aids for it, and very often the horse works better. This applies to when they are ridden and also when they are on a rein. It does sound a bit far-fetched, but in practice it often seems to work, especially as an accompaniment to other aids.

To try this with your own horse, first make sure your mind is quiet and positive. Then give your normal aids but also demonstrate to your horse what you'd like him to do. Give it time, keep trying—not too hard—and just see what happens. Being passively open-minded may also allow messages to come in to your mind from your horse, if you are quiet and calm.

The author once saw two horses appear to agree to gang up on another horse in their field. They were some way apart, and looking at each other. Then, at the same moment, they both trotted assertively toward another horse eating some favored clover and chased him off so they could eat it themselves. It appears as if they could only have communicated in thought pictures.

Above: This little pony has sensibly decided to get away from the stallion. He is not too worried, but is just being on the safe side.

Left: Exchanging breath is a common way horses have of communicating, with other animals and humans. Just be careful that you are sending out the right feelings, or you might be nipped.

Signs of discomfort and pain

Horses generally have a low pain threshold. In the same way as some people are tougher or more stoic than others, so are horses; and horses show pain in a variety of ways, some of which are subtle.

Signs of discomfort

An uncomfortable horse will appear irritable, a little upset, impatient, or generally out of sorts. Some may try to rid themselves of their problem. If a head collar is rubbing, a horse may rub his head; if a rug or blanket is uncomfortable, he may bite at it or rub his body.

A ridden horse will not perform well, becoming uncooperative or moving unusually as he tries to avoid the discomfort. He will also display resistance to his work.

Below: Rolling is healthy behavior in a fit horse, but it can indicate colic. If a horse rolls too near a fence, like this, he could get his legs caught.

Possible triggers

- Uncomfortable tack or clothing
- Dirt or debris underneath tack or clothing, which is then rubbed into the horse's skin
- Dirt and debris packed into his feet
- Insects creating distress or irritation
- Skin diseases creating extreme discomfort

Signs of pain

A horse that is in pain will change his behavior noticeably and may become violent. If he has colic (abdominal pain), he may paw the ground, sweat, groan, and roll frequently, often not shaking himself—as healthy horses do—when he gets up. A horse with mild to moderate head pain may press his head against a wall and groan. This type of pain can cause a horse to look really miserable and to sweat and groan. He may be very tense and may possibly tremble.

Stronger pain will result in a frightened horse that behaves violently (as in some cases of colic, twisted gut, or bad toothache), throwing himself around. He may groan and grunt, sweat, and appear very frightened.

Below: *An ill-fitting or badly fastened rug can rub against a horse's body or legs, irritating him intensely.*

Possible triggers

- Colic, possibly due to digestive problems from bad feeding practices or improper chewing due to neglected teeth, or as a reaction to stress. A twisted gut can be caused by a fall, or faulty diet and feeding practices.
- Diseased or broken teeth due to neglect, a kick, or being knocked in the head during a fall.
- Strangles, a disease involving a painful and sometimes abscessed throat.
- An undetected injury, even a fracture, as the result of an accident, fight, or fall.

Riding techniques

Some riding methods can cause horses pain. These include harsh use of the bit or spurs, spurs that break the skin, whipping, and working the horse in equipment that forces him into an unnatural posture.

What to do

Make sure your horse's tack and clothing are in good condition, clean, well-fitting, and comfortably adjusted. Learn about horses, and your own horse in particular, so that you know when something even very minor is not right and his behavior or demeanor has changed. Do not hesitate to ask someone caring and experienced to give an opinion. It is always best to call in your vet if you cannot solve a problem quickly.

Detecting lameness

Lameness is a puzzle to many owners as there are so many causes, but fortunately the main signs are not difficult to learn. These vary from the extremely obvious to the very difficult to discern, especially if a pair of feet are affected.

What is it?

Lameness is an altered or uneven way of the horse moving due to pain or discomfort in a foot or feet, or in a leg or legs. Sometimes swelling and heat are also involved. Horses lame in both feet of a pair may shift their weight from one foot to the other. Lameness always results in a shortening of the horse's normal stride, and a shuffling action if a pair of feet is involved. Lameness is gauged on a scale of 0–10, zero meaning no lameness at all and ten meaning that the horse cannot bear weight on the affected leg. Old injuries can become painless but permanently affect the horse's action. These cases are referred to as mechanical lameness and your vet should be consulted about suitable exercise to aid movement.

Possible triggers

Common causes of lameness are leg injuries, such as an overstressed and torn muscle, tendon, or ligament. If a horse has a fracture, he will almost certainly be lame and may not be able to put his foot on the ground.

An injury elsewhere in the body can cause lameness as the horse moves differently to try to avoid using the painful part. Back problems and pain in the shoulders or hindquarters are common examples.

Diseases such as arthritis (see pages 60–61) or laminitis (see pages 64–65) can cause lameness, as can infections such as lymphangitis or an abscess in the foot.

Lameness checks

If your horse is very lame, it will be obvious even in the stable. To check less marked lameness, walk and/or trot him in hand on a hard, even surface.

Foreleg lameness Get a helper to lead the horse straight toward you in a walk on a completely loose lead rope (so that his movement is not influenced), and watch for his head rising and dropping (see box). If nothing is obvious when walking, trot the horse, again on a completely loose rope.

Hind leg lameness Watch from behind as the horse is walked and/or trotted on a completely loose rope away from you, watching the levels of the points of his hips (see box). Walking the horse in a small figure eight on a loose rope and hard surface will reveal even slight discomfort. Do not lunge your horse on a hard surface as is sometimes suggested: this can be dangerous and make the problem worse.

What to do

Ask an experienced person if you are unsure about your horse's condition. Very slight lameness may right itself with twenty-four hours' stable rest. If it does not, call the vet. Anything worse needs immediate veterinary attention. Do not exercise the horse at all, and reduce or cut out concentrates (grains, pellets, coarse mixes). Feeding a nonworking horse can cause problems such as colic or laminitis, compounding your problems.

Headshaking

When your horse makes a seemingly involuntary, sometimes dramatic, toss of the head, it can be an extremely unnerving experience. Headshaking is a common condition, but one you should take seriously.

What is it?

Headshaking can refer to a horse tossing his head, sneezing, snorting, and rubbing his nose, possibly as though an insect has gone up his nostril. The horse is fairly out of control and can hit his rider in the face with his head. Sometimes it can be so extreme as to throw horse and rider off balance.

Possible triggers

Headshaking seems to be seasonal in about two-thirds of cases. This may indicate sensitivity to pollen, change in light or heat, or insect attack.

Scientific studies indicate that sudden stimulation of the trigeminal nerve in the head can result in reflex responses like those seen in headshakers, similar to a light-induced sneeze in humans. Damage to this nerve could be hereditary.

What to do

Most cases reflect a hypersensitivity or a reaction to pain, so be sure to address the problem and don't continue to ride your horse, hoping it will go away.

First make sure you can rule out obvious causes like insects. Check your horse's tack to ensure that the bridle isn't too tight or rubbing. If after this you are still unsure, call the vet, who will give your horse a thorough examination, checking for fungal infection and ear mites as well as inflammation or ulcers in the mouth.

Help your vet by keeping a diary, noting weather conditions and details of your horse's work when headshaking occurs.

Left: Headshaking can be mild or violent but the horse usually seems quite unable to control it or stop doing it.

Right: Sensitivity to insect irritation or to pollen can trigger headshaking. Sometimes wearing a fine mesh nose cover can help.

ASK YOURSELF

Does your horse shake his head only when outside?
➪ This could be a symptom of bright sunlight irritating the trigeminal nerve.

Does the headshaking stop once he's turned out?
➪ This may indicate that his bridle was too tight.

Has there been a seasonal change?
➪ Spring is the most common time for headshaking, which could indicate a reaction to light or pollen.

Are there any insects around his head?
➪ It could be an exaggerated response to flies and, in particular, to midges or wasps. Check also for mites, ticks, and debris, particularly in the ears.

Are there signs of external injury?
➪ Teeth and mouth problems are common causes of headshaking, but also check for sores or infected insect bites and wounds on the head.

Is it you?
➪ Get someone else to ride your horse while you watch. If he seems fine with other riders, ask a sympathetic teacher about how to prepare and ride your horse.

Is it worse when he is asked to come on the bit?
➪ This could indicate pain in the mouth, throat, or poll.

Shying and spooking

These actions on the part of the horse can be really unnerving for some riders. As prey animals, many horses are easily startled, sometimes by sounds, more often by sights, but also by something physical like an insect bite.

What are they?

Shy This is a sudden, sideways leap away from something that has startled the horse or something he does not like.

Spook This casual term has gained currency in recent years. It describes the behavior of a horse that is startled and showing any of the natural startle responses of ears pricked toward the problem, eyes wide and looking at it, stopping, snorting, head up, muscular tension, leaping about, and similar actions.

Above: *Company usually helps spooked horses, but not always. It is still worth trying as a possible solution.*

Right: *If a horse takes off away from something that has frightened him, sit with a firm, upright posture and speak to him to calm him and give him confidence.*

The horse's **eyesight** may be deteriorating, so he will be unable to assess objects or distances well. This will make him more nervous and wary. He may lose self-confidence, or confidence in his handler, rider, or driver. Ultimately, he may become unsafe to work. Nevertheless, in some cases blind horses that have a fully trusting relationship with their rider can work well for them. The owner/handler must keep all objects in the horse's environment in the same place, so the horse can find his way around with confidence.

Your **relationship** with your horse may require some improvement. Horses that shy and spook often are insecure and may have no confidence in the reassurance or protective abilities of the people who look after and work them. If the handler/ rider is not confident and competent, the horse will sense this.

Possible triggers

Both shying and spooking can be caused by something the horse regards as suspicious. This could be anything from clearly harmless (to us), like a plastic bag caught in the hedge, a sudden noise, or a large, noisy, fast vehicle on the road. The sight of something unfamiliar or in a different position can have the same effect. For example, garbage dumped on a familiar route constitutes a change in the environment, which could spell danger to the horse.

Shying and spooking behavior often results from habit. Horses form habits easily and have excellent memories. If a horse shies at the same place every time he passes it because something once startled him there in the past, he is operating from habit, memory, and expectation, not from concern or fear.

What to do

On the ground, you must have reliable control. Try handling a spooked horse in a humane controller halter. Buy a reputable design that comes with clear instructions on how to use it. Another method is to use a chain wound around the noseband of a normal head collar; you can use a heavyweight dog chain collar. Pass the rings on the ends through the head collar ring under the horse's jaw and clip your lead rope to them. Use it in quick tugs, not with sharp jabs or with a sustained pressure.

Under saddle, work on developing a secure, deep, and independent seat and ride the horse in a manner he respects but which is not harsh. Work on your attitude and your relationship with your horse so that his confidence improves and he feels safe in your company (see box).

Most horses are expected to work to some extent, and to work well and safely they must be physically and mentally fit. Fit horses generally have fewer health problems in the long term than soft (unfit) ones and, like fit humans, also feel better.

Fitness

FITNESS AND BEHAVIOR
Unfit horses that are made to work too hard become embittered, as they associate their work with discomfort and distress. This can cause behavioral problems such as refusing to leave the stable yard, becoming difficult to tack up, napping (balking) while on a ride, and other resistance problems under saddle. In addition, unfit tissues can be injured much more easily.

WEEKEND WARRIORS
A common question is: "My horse doesn't work hard. We just hack for a couple of hours weekends or in school in the arena. Surely he doesn't need to be fit?" Two-hour hacks and schooling are actually pretty demanding for a horse that does nothing else all week. If such horses cannot be ridden even once during the week, their weekend work needs to be light.

WHERE DO I START?
Start with two to four weeks of walking, on five or six days a week. Do not plan your horse's days off together, but split them up. The fitter you need him to be, the longer the walking phase should be. Gradually build up to walking briskly on a long rein but up to his bridle, without constantly nagging him, for up to two hours.

TROTTING
Next, introduce trotting, initially for just five minutes, building up over two weeks to the horse being able to do two twenty-minute trot periods per ride of two hours. A little easy jumping and arena work can be introduced toward the end of this period.

CANTERING
Now introduce short canters of a few minutes, then build them up until the horse can manage two bouts of five to ten minutes of steady cantering per ride on three days a week, at the end of six or eight weeks. More demanding jumping and arena schooling can be introduced now.

Your horse is now considered half-fit, provided there have been no setbacks such as injuries. If required, extend the program to ten or twelve weeks, introducing gallop stints in the same way.

VITAL SIGNS
Temperature, pulse, and respiration (TPR) rates are the vital signs that provide a useful, general guide to your horse's fitness. Measure these at the same time and under the same conditions every day for a week, to find his normal at-rest rates. Any good book on veterinary matters or fitness will provide details on how to do this.

Signs of discomfort or pain

The horse's behavior will almost certainly change, depending on his temperament and the severity of his discomfort or pain.

The horse may start moving and holding himself awkwardly even when not ridden. For example, he will often have great difficulty getting up or lying down, and may actually stop lying down to roll, rest, and sleep. He will not work as well as usual and he could be resistant or reluctant to work. Back problems are a common cause of refusing to jump.

When you approach with the saddle, the horse may look worried, move away, or drop his back. When you groom his back, he could react in the same way.

A sensitive horse or one that is in pain is likely to start bucking, playing up, or trying to run away. Nipping and fighting the rider can also occur. Going up or down slopes usually produces a reluctant horse. If you ask a horse with a back problem to go backward, he will often not be able to do so and will root his hind legs to the ground.

Possible triggers

- Acute (recent/short-lived) or chronic (longer-standing) injury due to bruising from the saddle or rolling on a stone, or torn soft tissue due to overstraining, usually work-related.
- The body somehow being out of alignment, maybe due to a fall, making movement difficult.
- A skin problem in the saddle/girth area causing pain or irritation on pressure from tack. This might include an insect sting or bite, a disease, an allergy, blocked sweat glands or, in some countries, insect larvae developing under the skin.
- The horse moving awkwardly due to pain or discomfort elsewhere, such as in the mouth, feet, or legs, leading to back strain. Using unaccustomed muscles to move so as to avoid pain in others stresses them and alters the horse's whole way of moving.
- A saddle that is poorly maintained (hard due to lack of care, or lumpy stuffing due to inadequate periodic checks), or one that fits badly or is placed wrongly (including the saddle pad or girth). All these can cause pressure and rubbing.
- Bad riding. People who ride crookedly or bang about cause pressure and jarring to the horse's spine and soft tissues, while those who overrestrict the head and neck force the horse to use his back in an unnatural way, which overstresses it.
- Unsuitable trimming or shoeing, which results in uncomfortable feet and compensatory movement. Being without shoes can also cause problems by making the horse footsore.

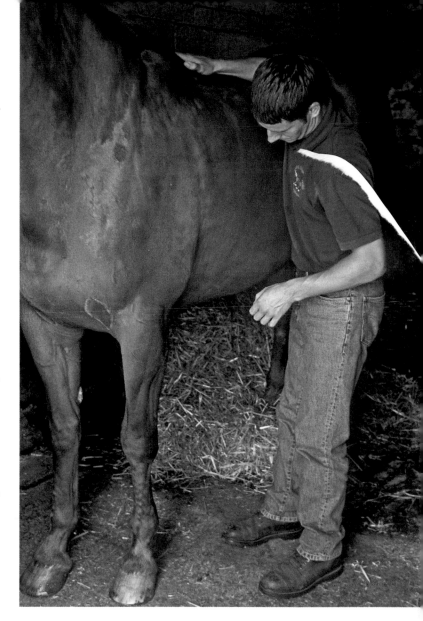

Above: *Veterinary surgeons and other qualified physical therapists can be a great help in treating back problems.*

Left: *A horse's back is just as susceptible to painful injuries as a human's. His problems are made worse because we sit on them.*

What to do

If the cause is not obvious, first check your horse's saddle and girth for good fit (see pages 52–53), and the skin in his entire saddle and girth area for swellings, bare or raw patches, or pain with pressure (just enough pressure to remove a patch of butter from a work surface). Check his bridle and bit for smooth conditions and good fit. Trot him up to see if he is actually lame, or moving or holding himself awkwardly.

You may need help in determining the situation, so do not hesitate to call in an expert such as your vet, saddle fitter, farrier, dental technician, or riding teacher.

Fitting saddles, bridles, and bits

Uncomfortable tack causes horses a good deal of distress, discomfort, and pain. It doesn't matter how good the quality or how much it costs—if it doesn't fit, it is useless, harmful, and may even be dangerous.

Left: *If you can fit the flat of your fingers under the front of a worn saddle, it probably fits well in this area.*

Right: *When a bit fits well, there is plenty of room around the base of the ears, the bit doesn't create any wrinkles, and the straps do not appear too tight.*

Signs of discomfort

A horse will almost always react to badly fitting tack by playing up, moving or holding himself awkwardly, working reluctantly, or refusing to work at all.

Basic correct saddle fit

A badly fitting saddle will cause discomfort or pain in the horse's back, which can result in bucking or a general reluctance to work.

- With the horse's heaviest rider mounted, the saddle must clear the spine by about 2 inches all along.
- It should lie with its front edge behind the tops of the shoulder blades behind the withers, so that you can fit the edge of your hand in between to avoid restricting the shoulders. The cantle should not reach beyond your horse's last rib.
- The panel under the seat must follow the shape of the horse's back and not cause uneven pressure.
- You should be able to slide the flat of your fingers fairly easily under the edges of the saddle all around. Too narrow and the saddle will pinch the horse; too wide and it will rock from side to side. Both cause bruising.
- The saddle pad must come outside the edges of the saddle so that there is no pressure on its binding. It should be smooth and clean, with no dirt or debris, especially on the underside, and be pulled right up into the saddle gullet to allow spine clearance.
- The girth must lie about a hand's width behind the horse's elbow to allow the forelegs to move freely. Ideally, it should be shaped to fit in this area.

Basic correct bridle fit

A badly fitting bridle will often cause the horse to toss or shake his head, and because he is uncomfortable, his work will suffer.

- You must be able to slide a finger easily under all the bridle straps all around your horse's head, including the noseband.
- The browband must not pull the headpiece into the ears or rub them itself, or flop about.
- The throatlatch should lie halfway down the round jaw bones for adequate throat clearance.

Basic correct bit fit

A badly fitting bit will cause the horse to resist the rider's rein aids, affecting control and safety as well as the quality of the horse's performance.

- A jointed mouthpiece should create no more than one wrinkle at the corner of the horse's lips.
- A nonjointed mouthpiece should fit snugly up to the corner of the lips without creating any wrinkles.
- In a double bridle, the bridoon (thin snaffle) fits as above, with the curb lying about ½ inch lower, and beneath it in the mouth.
- A curb chain must lie well down in the curb/chin groove and lie flat, not twisted.
- For correct width, you should just be able to fit the width of one finger between the corner of the horse's mouth and the bit ring or cheek.

ENSURING GOOD SADDLE FIT

Your saddle should be fitted and checked regularly by a qualified saddle fitter and maintained by a qualified saddler. Most good tack retailers employ saddle fitters. Horses' backs vary greatly in shape and there are many special types of saddles with adjustable gullets, flexible structures, air-filled panels, and other designs, each requiring their own specialized fitter.

Sweating

Like us, horses sweat all the time, but our sweat usually evaporates away from our bodies and into our clothes or the atmosphere before we notice it. Horses probably sweat more than any other animal.

What is sweat?

Sweat is a liquid excreted by the sweat glands in the skin through ducts or pores on the skin surface. It is an important way of ridding the body of waste and toxic substances, which are carried to the glands in blood through vessels (capillaries) that are one cell thick. Sweat also carries excess heat away from the body by evaporation, helping to keep the body temperature within healthy limits.

What triggers sweating?

Sweating occurs when the horse needs to lose heat while working, or when he is somewhere too hot (such as a stuffy stable or horsebox) or when he is wearing too many rugs. It also occurs in mild weather when the horse has a thick coat, and when a horse is excited, frightened, in distress, or suffering pain.

What to do

Sweating is a perfectly natural process, but you need to understand why your horse is sweating so you know whether or not to deal with it, and how.

If he has been working, he may become hot and sweaty, and you can help him to cool down. Judge the weather. If it is hot,

try to walk him in the shade and sponge him down with cool water, letting him drink a little water every ten minutes or so until he is cool. If it is cold, throw a rug over him as you walk him and let him drink, but do not sponge him down. You can groom him later, when he is dry.

If your horse sweats frequently and has a thick coat, he probably needs to be clipped. It is much harder for a horse to cool down than to warm up, and horses can suffer considerably when too hot. Do not clip him more extensively than necessary, though, and do not pile on too many rugs to compensate for the loss of his coat—a very common mistake. Your horse needs to be comfortably warm.

If his sweating is patchy and he seems agitated, your horse could be frightened and/or in pain. Cold sweats can indicate exhaustion or fear. You need expert help.

DEHYDRATION

Horses need to drink to replace fluid and replenish electrolytes (mineral salts) lost in sweat. An athletic, working horse can feel too tired to drink. Encourage him by syringing a little water into his mouth. He will drink more if the water is at a comfortable temperature, not too cold, so if you are at a competition, add a little hot water from a flask.

You can add electrolyte supplements to water, but offer your horse a choice of plain tap water as well because he may not like the taste of treated water. Whatever the case, he must drink, and you may need veterinary help if he refuses to do so.

To check for dehydration, press your thumb firmly on your horse's gum at the root of one of his corner teeth. The resulting pale patch should become pink again within a second or two, otherwise he could be dehydrated.

Far left: *Sponging down your horse with cool water will help him recover after hard work. This horse is performing the flehmen action, assessing the smell of the handler's sponge.*

Left: *Sweating after work is normal if the horse has worked hard and/or the weather is hot. He would benefit from shade if it's hot, or a rug if it's cold, and from a drink.*

Muscles, tendons, and ligaments

Injuries to muscles, tendons, and ligaments, and indeed most other soft tissues, are invariably painful. Even a slight injury can significantly affect your horse's behavior and reaction to movement, whether ridden or not. If a horse is worked with even a slight injury, it will get worse and is most unkind to the horse. Getting to know the look and feel of your horse's normal, sound action is crucial to your being able to tell when something is wrong.

Above: Losing his footing when galloping can easily tweak a horse's tendon.

Right: A good physiotherapist can be a real boon to any horse, working or resting, with her unique skills, trained eye, and touch.

What are injuries?

Injuries consist of tissue that has been torn and damaged due to overstress. If pressure or force is applied to a body part that is more than its tissues can stand, they will tear or become compressed (bruised) to the extent that their structure is damaged.

The tissues making up muscle, tendon, and ligament are well supplied with nerves, so injuries can be extremely painful. Inflammation, with its symptoms of heat and swelling, will be present to a greater or lesser extent depending on the severity of the injury, and arises when the cells are broken and fluids seep into the surrounding area. In addition, blood and lymph are channeled to the area to start the healing process by supplying oxygen and nutrients and removing damaged tissue.

Although inflammation is a natural healing mechanism, sometimes the body overdoes it, resulting in congestion around the injury. This prevents the free flow of blood and drainage of other fluids leaking out of damaged cells, both of which hamper healing. Swelling also causes pressure on nerve endings in the area, increasing the pain.

Possible causes

Injuries can happen almost anywhere, at any time, and under any circumstances—whether the horse is stabled, working, in the field, ridden or not. Horses can fall, take a misstep, slip and slide, become overworked, sustain kicks from other horses, strain themselves getting up, and more.

You cannot and should not overprotect your horse. You can take sensible precautions against injuries such as using leg protection, not turning enemies out together, not working a horse beyond his capacity, creating safe surroundings, and so on, but ultimately injuries are part of life with horses.

Signs of injury

Your horse will move differently as he tries to avoid using or putting weight on the painful part. He may be lame if a leg is involved, or may appear stiff, awkward, and tense if some other part is injured. He may not want—or be able—to lie down because of the pain and the difficulty of getting up again. He may be reluctant to let you touch the painful area.

What to do

Your vet will need to diagnose exactly where the injury is, its nature, and its extent, and will advise on treatment. Anti-inflammatory and painkilling medicines will probably be given. If the injury is accessible, such as on a leg, the horse may require support dressings and will certainly need rest to allow the area to heal properly. In the case of bad muscle injuries and sprained tendons and ligaments, this can involve many months off work.

It is worth asking your vet to refer you to a physiotherapist for treatment for this sort of injury, as suitable physical therapy can speed up the healing process. Your vet and physiotherapist should discuss the case with you and figure out a treatment plan.

COMPLEMENTARY THERAPIES

Nowadays, physiotherapy—with its advances in healing methods such as laser therapy, ultrasound, and others—is an integral part of healing equine injuries. In some countries, the law requires a physiotherapist or other therapist such as a chiropractor, osteopath, massage, or Bowen therapist to be referred by your vet, but if they do not suggest it, you can ask. Such treatment from a qualified, insured practitioner can enhance the healing process and, in some cases, speed recovery. Most insurance policies from reputable companies offer coverage for the services of these valuable experts.

Coat, mane, and tail

The color, type, and condition of a horse's coat, mane, and tail can have a tremendous influence on the first impression he creates on both people and other animals. They are also good indicators of his state of health.

WHAT IS THEIR FUNCTION?
A horse's coat, mane, and tail:
- Protect his skin.
- Help regulate his body temperature.
- Help protect him against the weather.
- Can act as camouflage.
- Can help in forming relationships, as horses of similar colors often herd together.

SEASONAL CHANGES
Horses change their coats twice a year, in spring and fall, but not normally their mane, forelock, and tail hair or any long hair (feather) around their fetlocks.

Coat change is decided mainly by the lengthening and shortening of days, but also by temperature and food availability. Once the winter solstice has passed, the brain registers more light entering the eyes, which triggers the production of hormones controlling coat growth. The horse starts to cast (molt) the thicker winter coat and grow the shorter summer one, casting a little and growing a little until the change is complete sometime during the spring. After the summer solstice, a similar process occurs to cast the summer coat and grow the winter one.

In parts of the world close to the equator, where there is little seasonal variation, horses' coats remain more or less the same all year round.

PROTECTION
Each hair in the horse's coat has a tiny muscle at its base that lifts it away from the skin. This creates a layer of warm air

THE COMMON INTEGUMENT
This term denotes the horse's skin, hair, and horn in hoof, chestnut (soft, hooflike material a few inches above the knee and below the hock) and ergot, (similar to the chestnut but tougher and on the rear underside of the fetlock joint). The very thin outer layer of skin, the hair, and the horn are all insensitive and made mainly from a hardened protein substance called keratin. Their health and quality are affected by the horse's diet; a poor diet will produce poor horn, dry skin prone to problems, and a duller, rougher coat. If the diet is improved, all three improve with it.

next to it to help insulate the horse. In warmer weather, the hairs lie flat. This effect can be destroyed by wind parting the hair and blowing the warmth away, and especially by rain or sweat, which flatten the coat and are good conductors of heat away from the body.

Hairs and skin are lubricated by a natural oil called sebum, which is secreted by glands in the skin. This helps make the coat and skin water-resistant. Overshampooing by a zealous owner removes this protection, which can dry out the coat and skin, and may cause skin problems. Rinsing with clear, warm water can be just as good.

GROOMING, CLIPPING, AND TRIMMING

It's understandable to want your horse to look good, but it's kinder to him to go easy on clipping and trimming. Clip only as much as is necessary to keep him comfortable; do not pull or clip the dock hair in horses that are turned out a good deal, as they need it for protection, and never clip off the feeler hairs around the muzzle and eyes, which are an important part of the horse's sensory equipment.

Grooming is needed to keep horses decently clean, to help maintain good skin health.

Left: Many people prefer long manes, but there's no denying that it takes a great deal of work to keep them looking good.

Below: A healthy coat is glossy and looks obviously well cared for.

Bones, joints, and nerves

Your horse's conformation, action, and performance depend on the structure, functioning, and health of his skeleton. It has to support not only the weight of the horse himself but also that of his rider and tack, which are increased by the force of movement.

Bone

Bone is made up of a collagen/protein matrix and bone cells, but about half its weight consists of calcium phosphate. It is made flexible by means of joints between bones and is softest in young animals, maturing in the horse's prime years, and then becoming more brittle in old age.

Breaks or fractures in bones do not present the death sentence they used to due to advances in veterinary science. Bone can become overstressed by working horses to their capacity repeatedly, with work on even ground in straight lines being the least stressful. Turns and circles involve uneven loading of weight, which stresses bone material much more. When an overload state arises, this can lead to a fracture.

What to do

Always feed your horse a professionally balanced diet to ensure that the bone acquires the necessary nutrients, particularly during youth and development. Study health and fitness, work your horse moderately and considerately, and contact your vet at the first sign of a problem such as altered gait, lameness, or swelling. Most good feed companies have free customer service, including qualified nutritionists to plan a suitable diet for your horse.

Joints

The skeleton is made flexible by means of joints between bones. Joints are sealed in a membranous sac, lubricated by joint oil (synovial fluid) and cushioned by cartilage, a gristly substance that covers the ends of the bones. The most common joint problem is arthritis of various kinds, which can end a horse's working life. This may be caused by wear and tear; poor diet; faulty shoeing and trimming, which can cause uneven weight-bearing and therefore stresses on the bones and joints; poor riding and way of going in the horse; and probably hereditary factors.

What to do

To help preserve bone and joint integrity, pay attention to the factors listed above. Many believe that hardworking horses and those from the age of about eight years and up should be given feed supplements containing glucosamine (which helps to maintain joint tissues) and other nutrients that seem beneficial. Check with your vet and nutritionist about other advances in prevention and treatment. If your horse is not moving as fluidly or, apparently, willingly as he used to, don't assume he is just a bit stiff. Get good advice from a qualified professional.

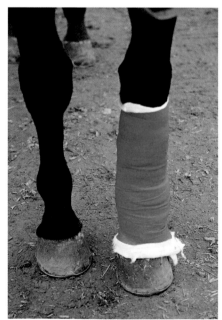

Far left: *Deformities in young foals can be due to incorrect feeding of the dam. Prevention by good feeding is better than surgery and special farriery later.*

Left: *Tendon and joint injuries often need support bandaging. It is a skill that requires practice, to ensure the bandage is at the correct tension.*

Right: *Your horse's movement is made possible by nervous impulses passing to and from his muscles and his central nervous system, causing his muscles, bones, and joints to move.*

Nerves

Nerves are extensions of the brain and spinal cord (the central nervous system, or CNS). They convey impulses between the CNS and other parts of the body. Sensory nerves convey sensations or feelings from various parts of the body to the CNS, and motor nerves convey messages to the body from the CNS—for example, telling the horse to move away from something unpleasant.

Nerves can be damaged by disease or injury. In the diagnosis of lameness, a vet may use a nerve block— an injection of anasthetic to desensitize a particular nerve to see if the lameness improves. This helps the vet decide which part of the leg, for instance, is affected so that he can make an accurate diagnosis. Sometimes a few nerve blocks are needed to pinpoint the appropriate nerve, but they are well worthwhile and a useful diagnostic tool. Of course, when the block wears off, your horse will become lame again.

What to do

Because the horse's nervous system controls many bodily activities, you should be ready to report any signs of abnormal behavior to your vet. These may be due to nervous problems or other causes, but veterinary treatment should not be delayed.

Common signs of nerve problems include paralysis of small or large parts of the body, wandering, lack of coordination, staggering, loss of consciousness, malfunction of any kind, weakness and poor development of any part of the body, unexplained signs of pain, stumbling, falling, and strange movements, postures, or gaits.

Nerve damage is potentially serious and the outlook for recovery not always good. It can be caused by accident, injury, and disease, but repeatedly making a horse work in a bad posture, such as holding his head and neck in too much, can also cause it. This alone is an excellent reason for allowing a more natural posture.

Shivering

Shivering can be the normal muscle action that animals and people make involuntarily to keep warm, or it can be due to nerve damage. Seeing your horse in this state can be confusing and worrying if you don't know the cause.

Right: Well-fitting turnout rugs are great, provided they are comfortable and do not make a horse too hot.

Below: A thick winter coat will keep a horse happy on a snowy day.

What is it?

Shivering due to low temperatures is a reaction of the body, causing the muscles to twitch rapidly in an effort to create heat. If the horse feels cold, he will shiver all over, sometimes quite violently, as his body tries to warm up.

Shivering in the hind legs and tail, and occasionally the forelegs, is probably due to damage to the nerves supplying them. A vet will diagnose this by flexing the legs and pulling to the side. On returning to the ground, the leg will shiver—sometimes quite violently—and the tail will rise and quiver. In advanced cases, the shivering may occur when the horse tries to lift his hind legs to move backward.

Possible triggers

Shivering due to cold Horses feel the cold less than humans, but this does not mean they are immune to it. They are very susceptible to wind and rain, especially when both occur at the same time. Drafty stables and exposed situations even in cool weather can make them feel cold. Letting your horse stand around in a draft, breeze, or wind in cold weather when he is wet from sweat, rain, or washing will chill him.

Shivering due to disease This is probably due to nerve damage, but hereditary factors may cause a horse to be susceptible. It is a progressive disorder that conventional veterinary medicine seems little able to do anything about.

What to do

Shivering due to cold Check whether your horse is warm or cold by laying the flat of your hand on his ears, neck, sides, and hindquarters. If he feels cold, decide whether he is in a draft or if it is just a cold day. Do whatever you can about the draft and put a rug on him, maybe two if he is actually cold and shivering. Rubbing him down briskly with straw or towels will stimulate his skin and warm him up.

Make sure your horse is dry, warm, and calm before you leave him, and has plenty of fiber (hay) and water available. Eating fibrous food around the clock keeps horses warm for hours, as it produces slow-release energy.

Shivering due to disease Bear in mind that this is progressive and the horse is classed as unsound. Due to the instability it causes, such horses should not be worked. Discuss with your vet whether or not the horse could be in pain and administer appropriate painkillers or whatever other medicine might be helpful. Eventually, the horse will be unable to live a safe life even in the field and should be put down.

It may be worth asking complementary therapists whether they can help. Herbalism, homoeopathy, and/or acupuncture may be appropriate, although nerve damage is notoriously difficult to treat. In some countries, you need to get a referral from a veterinary surgeon to have a complementary therapist treat your horse, but they can be a valuable addition to your horse's healing regime and health maintenance.

Laminitis

Many owners are devastated when they learn that their horse has laminitis, and rightly so. Even when mild, this is one of those emergency situations in which time is of the essence if the horse is to make a good recovery.

What is it?

The laminae are sensitive strips of tissue on the outside of the pedal bone (foot bone, also called the coffin bone), which interleave with the insensitive ones lining the inside of the horny hoof wall. This extremely strong bond bears the whole of the horse's—and sometimes the rider's—weight. The horse is actually slung inside his feet by means of this bond, rather than his entire weight being borne on the sensitive inner sole of the foot.

In laminitis, this bond is at least partially destroyed so that the pedal bone becomes detached at the front of the foot (known as founder) and sometimes, more seriously, all around (when the horse is known as a sinker). It is caused by a disruption to the blood flow inside the foot. Blood is necessary to service the sensitive tissues, delivering oxygen and nutrients and removing waste products. If there is little or no blood supply, the tissues break down and separate from the insensitive laminae. The pedal bone becomes unstable and detaches from the inside of the hoof wall, causing excruciating pain. It often tilts downward at the toe, causing long-lasting soundness problems.

Possible triggers

Overeating is a common trigger for laminitis and the most familiar one, but it can also be triggered by jarring to the feet, illness, stress, certain medications, and anything that disturbs or changes the blood chemistry. The key trigger is an interruption to the normal blood flow to the sensitive laminae early in the development of the condition. The longer the tissues are without a normal blood supply, which could mean as little as a few hours, the less chance there is of recovery.

Symptoms

The horse will be in more or less pain depending on the severity of the condition. Often, horses get laminitis in both front feet, but they can get it in the hind feet, and in only one foot.

The horse will be footsore, puttering in his gait, and perhaps standing back on his heels to take the weight off the painful toe area. He may wave a foot in the air (a sign of great pain), paddle from one foot to the other, be reluctant to move, will probably lie down more, and may be unwilling or unable to get up. He may show patchy sweating or may groan, both of which are signs of pain.

What to do

Call your vet immediately if you suspect laminitis, no matter the day or time. Get your horse onto soft standing (deep bedding, soft soil or sand, with no access to grass), with clean water but no food at all, and wait for the vet to arrive.

The vet may advise frog supports for the underside of the feet, painkilling medication, and a restricted diet. Starvation is not appropriate and can make the disease worse. Laminitics need correctly balanced vitamins and minerals and restricted levels of feed designed specially for them.

Many feed companies now make feeds for laminitis-prone animals. The trick is to spread the ration out in several smaller portions than previously, so the body never becomes overloaded with food—but the horse should not become too hungry. The digestive system adjusts to less, and the appetite decreases.

Many of these special feed supplements marketed for animals prone to laminitis sound like lifesavers, implying that your horse or pony can still graze freely while taking them. Check with your vet and an independent nutritionist about the feasibility of this. They may well help greatly, but it is not a good idea to just carry on as though your horse were not laminitic. Some of the companies that make supplements have on their staff professionals such as medical herbalists or vets who have been trained specifically in clinical nutrition (nutrition as therapy), so speak to them and make sure you get a thorough understanding of how these supplements work.

Left: A heart-bar shoe is used to support the tip of the pedal bone inside the foot and greatly ease the animal's pain.

Below: This horse is standing in the classic laminitis stance, avoiding putting weight on his toes. However, this stance is not always present in laminitics.

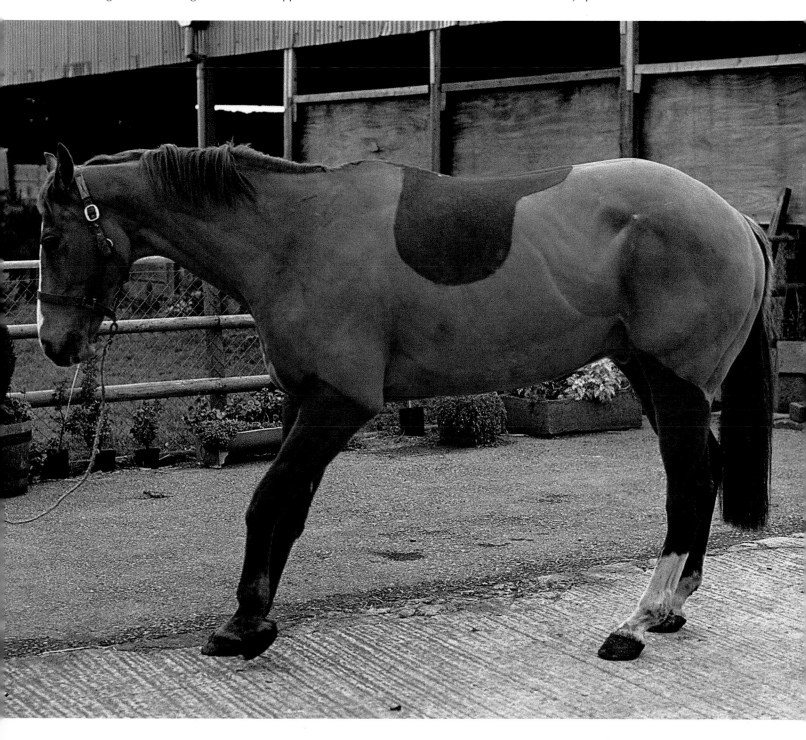

STABLE MANNERS

Few things are more irritating—or even intimidating—to deal with than a horse with no stable manners. Although the stable is the horse's space, for safety's sake he must respect the presence of people in it.

The term "stable manners" denotes the way a horse behaves toward people in his stable. Some horses seem to treat us with respect but others have no concept of manners. Yet others are positively dangerous because they are aggressive, defensive, or simply untrained. With all horses, much depends on how they have been treated in the past and therefore how they have learned to react to us.

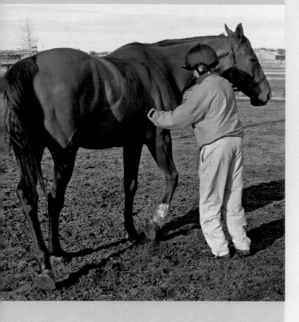

The well-mannered horse

A well-mannered horse will step back from the stable door when you enter or leave, and give you plenty of room. He will move sideways when you say "Over," maybe with a hand on his side. He will move forward when you say "Walk on" and backward when you say "Back." Most importantly, he will stand still when you say "Stand." He never tries to nip, kick, or crowd you.

A GOOD TRAINER
Assuming your horse has been taught to lead politely in hand and is not completely green (unschooled), training him in stable manners is not difficult. It is always helpful to have a good relationship with him, but taking even a few moments to get to know a strange horse will pay dividends.

DANGEROUS HORSES

If a horse is actually dangerous and is liable to bite, kick, corner, or squash you, leave a head collar on him. An experienced horse handler can encourage him to the door to accept a carrot and, as he is taking it, clip the lead rope on so that he can be tied up short to be cared for. Remember that horses can kick forward, sideways, and backward. In this scenario, it is important to get professional help as a matter of urgency.

A good horse person has certain qualities that really get through to horses. If you think you don't have them, tell yourself over and over again that you do. See yourself schooling your horse in this persona, and you will quickly find that it happens. Breathe calmly and deeply and tell yourself often that you are:
- Calm, quiet, and psychologically strong.
- Confident, firm, and quietly determined.
- Positive and upbeat—you expect your horse to cooperate.

Training for good manners
Horses tend to move away from intermittent pressure. Therefore, to get your horse to:

Move sideways away from you, bring his head toward you slightly and tap him firmly but not hard on the shoulder, side, or thigh with your hand, the end of your thumb, or a whip and continue giving one or two taps per second until he moves. The instant he moves away, stop tapping; he will associate moving away with the removal of the irritation.

Move back, tap his chest using the same principle, or give little backward tugs on his head collar. The idea is that he moves back to avoid the intermittent pressure on his chest or nose. As he does so, say "Back" so that he associates the word with the action.

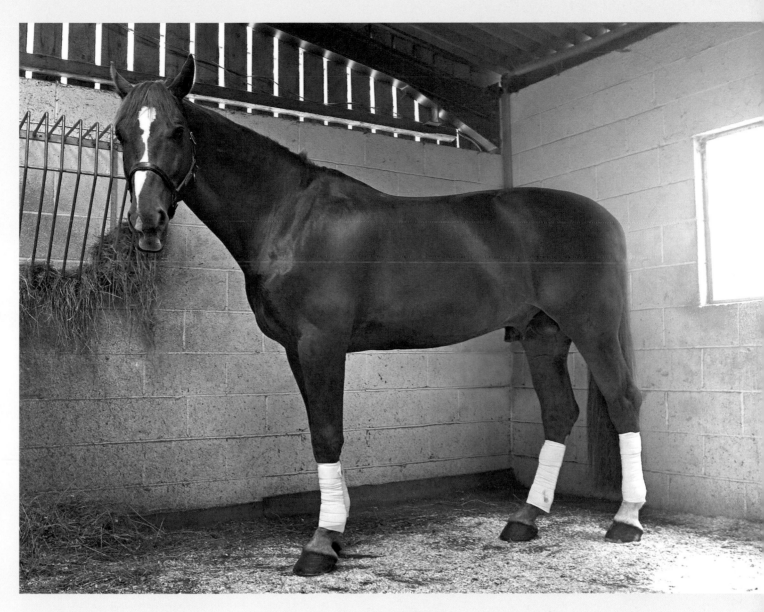

Move forward, hold his head collar and say "Walk on." As he already leads in hand, he will understand this. If he isn't wearing a head collar, pat him on the root of his tail. Once your horse's reactions are reliable, say the appropriate wordas soon as he starts to move. Pretty soon you'll be able to touch him and speak, and he will move. **Stand still,** position him where you want and say "Stand." The instant he moves away, say "No" sternly but without anger, put him back where he was, and say "Stand." Repeat until he obeys. As he stands, even for only a second or two, praise him by saying something he recognizes, such as "Good boy," and stroke his neck near the withers, which most horses like.

It can take a lot of patience to train horses in this way. Many people lose their tempers and hit the horse as a punishment when he does not obey, thinking they're teaching him a lesson. Horse minds do not work like human minds, and it is more effective to teach them along the lines just explained.

The horse must make a link between your vocal or physical aid (command or touch) and performing the action you want. When learning, he can only do this if you say the word as he does it, otherwise he will not learn to behave as you wish wit consistency.

Above: Horses have to be taught what we consider good manners. A well-behaved horse will stand back from the door as you enter the stable.

Left: Tapping a horse gently with on-off pressure from your hand is part of teaching him to move sideways.

Claustrophobia

Many people seem to believe that horses are naturally claustrophobic. In practice, it seems that most aren't. As creatures of wide-open spaces, however, it is not particularly surprising that a few are.

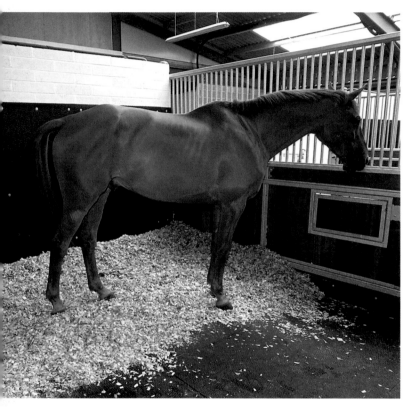

Possible triggers

Being in an enclosed space—particularly being shut in with no means of escape—can trigger the panic and fear of claustrophobia to susceptible horses (and people). Horses that have always lived outside and are suddenly stabled can show signs that could be taken for claustrophobia, but with consideration they usually adapt in due course. Others, perhaps those that are truly claustrophobic, may not.

Horses that are herded together with unfamiliar horses can show the same signs. Such situations can happen at markets, horse shows, small paddocks at establishments with changing populations (such as dealers' or livery yards), and in any other situation where strange horses are crowded together.

Even if a claustrophobic horse adapts, with or without help, he may never be completely at ease but will always display a certain level of tension. Some horses may release this tension by developing stable vices (see pages 82–91) as a means of relief from their distress.

What is it?

Claustrophobia is fear of enclosed spaces and of being shut in. Affected horses show any of the normal signs of fear and panic when closed in or in crowded situations. Some signs include wild eyes, snorting, tension, sweating, and kicking at the perimeter walls or fences.

Sometimes the fear may be due to the horse having experienced something painful or traumatic in a similar situation in the past, and not to claustrophobia itself. For example, if such an experience has taken place in a particular stable or yard, the horse will often be quite calm in a different one, so it could be worth moving him around.

They may also start box-walking, weaving, crib-biting, or wind-sucking. These are all behavioral abnormalities that used to be called "stable vices" but which are now more correctly considered stereotypical behaviors or stereotypies caused by distress (see pages 82–91).

What to do

Much depends on the life you want your horse to live, which may not be the same as the life he wants to live.

If your horse has always lived outside but is now destined to be stabled often and/or transported, you may have to spend a long time getting him very gradually accustomed to having his freedom curtailed. You can try to do this by putting him in progressively smaller enclosures, introducing open field shelters, putting him in stables with the door open, and so on, until he copes better—bearing in mind that he may never learn to cope and may subsequently need to live outside more or less permanently.

For a horse that is mildly affected, provide as large, light, and airy a stable as you can, ideally where he can come and go into an attached pen (see pages 94–95). High ceilings and a wide view of the surroundings can help. In transport, try different vehicles (horsecars are usually preferred to trailers). Some horses settle better if they can see out.

Above: Being able to see out of the stable, even through glass, helps some claustrophobic horses.

Left: A light and airy stable can give a horse a good view and good ventilation, both of which will help prevent claustrophobia.

THERAPIES TO TRY

Behavioral and psychological problems of various types are often helped by the TTeam-TTouch comprehensive method of therapy and management. Some claustrophobic people have been helped by homoeopathy, and your vet should be able to refer you to a homoeopathic vet who may be able to help your horse.

Separation anxiety

This is a distressing and common problem, and perhaps one to be expected in a herd animal like the horse. It can be difficult to deal with and some owners never try, ending up having to take two animals everywhere.

What is it?

Separation anxiety is the emotion horses feel when separated from their friends, often those with whom they have a close relationship, even though other horses are around. The horse will be very agitated and run around his paddock or stable, or stand by the gate, door, or window looking for his friend. He will probably neigh loudly and may kick at the door and walls, continually run up and down the fence, and possibly try to escape any way he can, from pushing through hedges to jumping over fences and even stable doors.

Horses are herd animals, born to be together, so this kind of anxiety is to be expected. However, they are very adaptable and can learn to accept separation for limited periods of time. At these times, the company of some other kind of animal can help greatly. Some horses form friendships with cats, dogs, goats, or hens, but make sure that they get along well before leaving them together.

GOOD-BYE FOR NOW!

Horses that are strongly bonded can gradually become accustomed gradually to being handled and worked further and further apart over a period of weeks or even months. The important thing is for the handlers and riders to remain strong, quietly determined, and upbeat.

In-hand and ridden schooling must be continued to establish obedience and relaxation as habits. Ignore calling and carry on as though you expect your horse to cooperate, praising him when he does. It is important that you are able to gain your horse's attention, and regain it whenever he becomes distracted. Use his name frequently so that he learns it, and then you can use it when you want his attention.

Do not praise your horse as a calming measure; if he understands the praise words, he will think you are praising him for becoming upset and playing up.

Possible triggers

A horse that has just changed homes may be remembering his former companions and, although other horses are around, can display anxious behaviors. These will almost certainly subside with time as he settles in.

Certainly, separating close friends can trigger separation anxiety, although horses often improve once they realize that they will be reunited. If one is left at home for a while, providing other company such as a small pony as a nanny will often calm him down.

When the one taken away is calling to his friend and not working well, it is important for the rider to be strong, quiet, and firm, and ignore the calling. Turning around and coming home as soon as the horse starts calling or playing up will create an association in his mind; playing up equals returning to his friend. This is most definitely not what you want.

What to do

It is extremely inconvenient for us and potentially dangerous to horses for them to behave as described above. Also, in most domestic situations, a horse must accept working alone and being without his friends temporarily.

It certainly helps when the people dealing with the horse have a strong, calm, and kind way of handling him. The idea is for you, the human, to become an important, trustworthy member of your horse's herd, someone with whom he feels safe and is used to obeying. You must establish control in a firm, humane way, maybe with professional help, so that the horse comes to realize that nothing bad happens in your company and he will see his friend again soon. Try taking one horse a little distance from his friend, perhaps grooming him for a while, then returning him. Gradually making the absences longer and more regular often teaches tolerance, particularly if someone responsible stays with the other horse.

Biting

Biting can range from a painful little nip to a savage bite delivered with meaning. Most horses bite in self-defense due to previous bad treatment, and it can be difficult to cure.

What is it?

The signs that a horse plans to bite are ears pressed hard back and down, an angry look in his eyes, muzzle extended toward his intended victim, and front teeth bared, often with the mouth actually open. His tail might thrash—although you probably won't be looking at his back end! Mares are just as capable of biting as stallions or geldings.

In horse society, biting is both aggressive and defensive, and is a clear "go away" sign. Normally, the only animals that fight seriously are rival stallions, although skirmishes among others are seen. Youngsters often practice in this way for times when they may need to defend themselves.

Possible triggers

Horses are not naturally aggressive, but are pretty good at defending themselves. Biting is an effective defensive behavior, usually learned because a horse has been treated badly and people have hurt and injured him. Some less-knowledgeable handlers regard inflicting pain as punishment, but horses do not see things that way and naturally defend themselves. The biting behavior becomes well ingrained in the horse's mind and is established as a habit. Some horses develop the habit into putting their ears back and threatening to bite almost anyone who approaches them, or even actually attacking people they dislike and whom they feel they can dominate. They have then become dangerous.

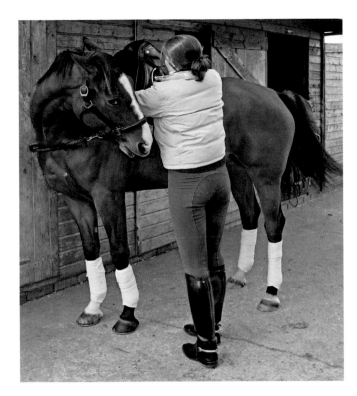

What to do

For long-term success, the horse needs retraining by a professional behaviorist well versed in learning theory and practice. As you may have discovered, hitting and shouting at a horse that bites is completely ineffective and merely confirms the horse in his behavior. It is essential that those dealing with a biter never lose their temper but remain cool, calm, and quick-witted.

There are some short-term techniques that can help create an unpleasant association with biting in the horse's mind. These must be carried out instantly and without fail every time he tries to bite for their message to start overriding his habitual behavior:

1. When the horse comes at you to bite, squirt him firmly on the muzzle with plain, cold water from a water pistol or garden hose. Alternatively, you could throw a bucket of water in the horse's face, but this is not as easy to do and is certainly more messy.
2. Sew bristle dog-grooming mitts on the upper sleeves of an old coat or sweatshirt and wear it when you groom or handle the horse, so that he experiences an unpleasant pricking sensation when he makes contact with them.

These sorts of techniques seem to be more effective if you do not look at or speak to the horse when you are using them. This way, most horses do not appear to make the connection between the unpleasantness and you, so no ill feeling is created.

As biting is so potentially dangerous, it is well worth asking your vet for a referral to a behavioral therapist, or engaging one who has been well recommended. Their techniques may not be for amateurs, but are often humane and successful.

DON'T TAKE CHANCES

It is tempting to try to develop trust by not tying up a biter as you work around him. However, until the horse has been correctly retrained and the behavior eliminaed, this can be very dangerous, so tie the horse up short for the meantime. Also bear in mind that the horse may never be completely cured.

Left: A horse will bite another horse, even one from his own herd, to tell him to go away.

Above left: Being roughly saddled up, or remembering past discomfort from it, can cause a horse to nip.

Kicking

Horses use kicking mainly as a defensive action, but also as an aggressive one and as a means of expressing frustration, usually at finding themselves in a situation they can do nothing about.

Right: It is standard practice to put a red ribbon in the tail of a horse who kicks, as a warning of his dangerous tendency.

Below: Dogs can inflict nasty injuries on horses, but—even if only as a defensive action—a horse's kick can kill a dog.

What is it?

A horse lifts one or both hind legs off the ground and kicks out, hard and fast, at anything annoying him, whether it is another horse, an animal, or a person. A kicking horse can kill whatever is on the receiving end and, at least, easily break bones. In fact, a horse can crack a brick wall with one kick, albeit at risk of injury to his feet, legs, and back.

Horses can also kick sideways and forward (known as cow-kicking), and experienced kickers are excellent at hitting their targets. Sensible people steer clear of unfamiliar horses' hind feet until they know them better.

Kick threats also occur quite commonly as a warning. The legs and feet are not extended out far and the horse may back toward his target. Unfortunately, it is impossible to tell whether or not the horse means to kick or only threaten, so any such action must be taken seriously.

Possible triggers

The obvious reason why horses kick is to remove an animal or person from their vicinity. This can happen when the horse is ridden (when he should have a red ribbon tied in his tail to indicate that he may kick), in harness, being led, in the field, or in the stable.

Horses that kick their stable walls normally do so at a neighbor they dislike or do not know, but this can become a stereotypic behavior (see pages 82–83) or a habit in time, and can continue when there is no horse in the stable next door, or even at one the horse likes. Such a horse may not only damage the structure of the stable but also himself.

Kicking is also a sign of frustration, usually at confinement in a stable or small enclosure, or some other distressing situation from which the horse cannot escape, such as activity in the yard, a friend being taken out, being transported, when in harness, being cornered by a horse or person, or when anxious about a horse or person approaching.

Horses will also kick up at their bellies to remove biting flies, and at abdominal pain, such as colic (see pages 36–37).

What to do

As kicking is a sign of a negative emotion, you must try to improve the horse's life and therefore his overall feeling of well-being. A basic need is the freedom to spend several hours a day socializing normally, at liberty with his friends. He needs a diet that provides no more energy than he requires, maybe of a calming nature, with ample fiber so that he does not become hungry and upset; constant clean water; and comfortable bedding. This will not stop him from kicking but should make him feel less like doing it.

If possible, the horse's work should be increased sensibly, so that he is occupied and healthily tired, and he should be given work he enjoys and of which he is capable. He must be treated well and competently by his handlers.

The horse's stable should be as large as can be provided, with tough padding fixed to the walls to lessen any blows and views out of more than one outlet, to keep his hind feet away from the walls and provide him with interest. Make certain that the horse's neighbors are his friends, and most certainly not his enemies.

Remember that horses can kick backward, forward, and sideways. Be very alert when working around a kicker. Tie him up and watch his back legs carefully! Try never to go directly behind him. Also, if he can work comfortably without shoes, consider having him unshod behind.

EXPERT HELP

Kicking can be very dangerous, so if your horse is exhibiting this behavior, you should seek expert help from a remedial therapist who is trained in dealing with these behaviors.

Eating and drinking disorders

Horses naturally spend about two-thirds to three-quarters of their time eating and, apart from those naturally caused by dental problems, eating disorders are not apparent in feral horses.

What are they?

Eating disorders include problems such as eating bedding, kicking and pawing while eating, throwing food around the stable, refusal to eat, and bolting or gobbling food. There are also those caused by dental problems such as quidding (dropping food out of the mouth), and bad chewing habits due to worn, uneven, sharp, or broken teeth (see pages 42–43).

Possible triggers

Behaviors approaching violence, such as pawing and kicking when eating, showing aggression at feed time, and throwing food around, are probably caused by the way we feed horses, forcing them into a pattern of eating that is nothing like their natural one.

Horses living naturally forage almost constantly for food they like, and which is always available under their feet. We take away that freedom, controlling not only their diet but also when (and whether) they are given food or allowed to graze. In addition, although we provide hay, it is often not a constant supply, and illogically we feed horses separate meals like we ourselves eat. All this is completely inappropriate for a free-grazing animal like a horse. No wonder some of them develop eating disorders.

The main cause of death in feral horses where predation does not exist is starvation because the teeth overgrow and become sharp, do not meet evenly, or become abscessed, broken, and diseased, and the mouth becomes very painful. Horses' teeth erupt through the gum and are worn down throughout their lives until they are down to the softer roots, which cannot grind down normal fibrous food or grain. Sometimes, food accumulates between the back teeth and the cheek, which the horse cannot remove. You can feel this from the outside, and need to carefully remove it with the long handle of a wooden spoon, or a similar tool.

What to do

Get a nutritionist to design a palatable, healthy, balanced diet with a low enough energy content to enable your horse to eat almost constantly without becoming overnourished. He will not then experience the frustration, discomfort, and distress of becoming hungry (an unnatural state for a horse), and will eat much more calmly.

Treat dental services as a major priority for your horse's health. Young and old horses need dental checks two to three times a year and those in midlife once or twice a year (see pages 42–43).

Feed your horse from a natural angle—as low as possible to the ground. This enables the lower jaw to drop forward naturally and allows more even tooth wear, more comfortable eating, and better digestion.

Ideally, abandon separate meals. Give your horse several containers around his stable, holding different types of fiber, from hay to short-chopped forage feeds, and scatter any concentrates (grains, pellets, coarse mixes) through the latter. Then he will have a consistent, varied diet almost constantly available as he needs it, with no high points (feed times) to wait for or become excited about.

DRINKING PROBLEMS

These may occur because:

- The horse is wary of his water container.
- He has a problem tooth that is sensitive to cold water.
- His container is too high for comfort.
- His water is not clean enough.
- He does not like the noise made by an automatic drinker, preferring a bucket or tub.

The answer to all these situations is obvious. Act quickly to correct them because a plentiful supply of clean water is crucial to a horse's well-being, health, and survival.

Above: *Many horses like playing with water, but if this becomes a habit and the horse fails to drink regularly, there is something wrong.*

Left: *If you offer a horse food you know he likes and he does not accept it, it could well be that he has a problem in his mouth.*

Door banging

One of the most annoying habits displayed by some stabled horses is banging the stable door with their front feet. Generally regarded as attention-seeking behavior, this is extremely annoying to people, damaging to the stable, and injurious to the horse. It can, of course, indicate that the horse wants to come out.

What is it?

This is a rhythmic banging of the stable door by the horse, using a front hoof. A common response from his attendants is to yell at the horse to stop it, which is, perhaps unsurprisingly, not very effective.

Apart from often damaging the door and doorjamb, horses can badly injure their legs and feet with this practice, and can end up with serious bruising or fracturing.

Possible triggers

Door banging is a sign of frustration, usually at being confined or left short of food. Other causes can be general discomfort (irritating rugs, for example), the sight of a friend going away, other horses being turned out, and lack of routine, so that the horse never knows what to expect. Equally, if an established, strict routine is ever broken, so that feed or turnout time is late by even a few minutes, this too can trigger door banging.

Unfortunately, when the horse's habits have become confirmed, door banging can be extremely difficult to prevent and may even take on the status of a stereotypic behavior (see pages 70 and 83–91), giving the horse a release from a situation he is helpless to improve. There is also the commonly held view that most horses who bang their door get some sort of attention from humans, even if it is negative, and this may be what they want because things are not right in their lives.

What to do

Door bangers that are kept with compatible stable mates, and those that are comfortable (this includes not being hungry, thirsty, or irritated by clothing), well-established in a routine and management system that suits them, and generally content do not bang their doors as much. Owners and carers need to try hard to understand why a horse is banging, taking note of his situation and what is happening in the yard when he starts doing it.

- If the horse bangs only when a friend is removed from the stable, try to exercise them both at the same time but not necessarily together.
- If the horse clearly does not like being stabled too much, change his management so that he can be outside more, maybe on a surfaced area with hay, water, and compatible company if grazing is not possible.
- Consider whether his rugs are really necessary and, if so, check that they are absolutely comfortable, not pulling tight or otherwise irritating him.
- Make sure that he has suitable food and clean water available nearly all the time.
- Observe him closely to see whether he prefers a quiet environment or a busier one.

If the horse really has to be stabled, albeit as little as possible,

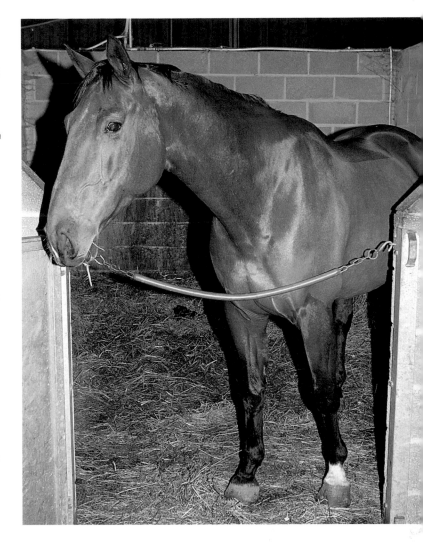

leave his door open and keep him inside by means of a chain or webbing mesh across the doorway. If he then pounds the floor in the doorway, fix thick rubber matting to the floor to cushion his hooves.

Some people recommend keeping the stable door shut and fitting a bar to it projecting about twelve inches into the stable, thereby preventing the horse from getting near enough to the door to bang it. However, he will probably simply stand behind it, pawing the ground.

Above: *The practice of clipping a rope or chain across the doorway keeps some horses from kicking, but others simply paw the ground instead.*

Left: *Some horses will paw the ground if they have no door to bang. This horse, although not stabled, is pawing because he is tied up and wants to be freed.*

Stable vices

Although we have known for many years that behaviors formerly called "stable vices" result from inappropriate management and are not the horse's fault, there is much resistance to changing our attitudes. Today, the correct term for stable vices is stereotypies or stereotypic behaviors. So far, no satisfactory cure has been found for any of them, but their incidence can be reduced simply by making the horse happier.

WHAT ARE THEY?
Stereotypies are repetitive, consistently similar, and apparently pointless actions. Many horse people will recognize such behaviors as crib biting, windsucking, weaving, and boxwalking, but there are many others, listed in the box below.

The fact that these have been known as vices betrays human thinking that the horse is doing something we find unwelcome and is therefore behaving badly. This attitude has been responsible for the barbaric methods people have employed to try to prevent the behaviors.

WHY DO THEY OCCUR?
Most scientists working in the field of behavior believe that stereotypies are the result of a horse being or having been kept in a way he finds unbearably distressing. The stereotypy he develops is believed to be a coping mechanism that gives him some relief from circumstances he feels helpless to control or escape. Stereotypies have been described as comfort behaviors or habits, to which horses may still resort even when their original cause has been removed.

The rocking back and forth of disturbed, traumatized people, cage pacing of confined zoo animals, and bar sucking of captive pigs are all similar behaviors with probably similar root causes: frustration and distress. The old cause quoted was boredom, which showed some insight but nothing enough to describe the real psychological damage done to horses that display stereotypical behaviors. Some people still do not accept this.

STEREOTYPIC BEHAVIORS

- Crib biting
- Windsucking
- Boxwalking
- Weaving
- Tongue lolling
- Licking lips and the surroundings
- Wood chewing
- Scraping teeth on stable door
- Pawing
- Kicking stable door and walls
- Self-mutilation
- Abnormal movements of head (twirling, shaking, nodding, circling, and similar movements)

Far left: The marks on this door have been caused by its occupant scraping his teeth from side to side over the door.

Left: Tongue lolling is another form of stereotypical behavior and a sign of inappropriate management, past or present.

WHAT TO DO

It has always been clear that, even where the root cause of a stereotypy has been known, removing that type of stimulus from the horse's environment does not stop the behavior. Chemical, physical, and surgical means of preventing horses from performing their behavior have never produced lasting results, and the current professional view is that you should make the horse as content as possible, giving him plenty of interest, constant and varied forage, amenable company, lots of turnout with friends, and absolutely minimal frustration and distress. This should reduce the performance level of the stereotypy, which you then have to accept. Punishing a horse for performing his behavior is unsuccessful, ill-advised, and cruel.

It is also most important not to prevent the horse from physically performing his stereotypies (many have more than one), as denying him this way of coping may well be contrary to his welfare. Do not isolate the horse; this will cause him more distress and, in any case, stereotypies are not contagious, as was previously thought. Certain horses develop them because they are susceptible to them under adverse circumstances, not through copying others. Keeping a horse calm and appropriately managed works best.

In the very early stages, you should be able to prevent a new stereotypy from taking hold by improving the horse's management. Calming feed additives and bodywork therapies such as shiatsu help many horses.

Crib biting and windsucking

These two common and similar stereotypies greatly irritate many owners because of the grunting noise that accompanies them both. Owners may also be worried about possible digestive problems, loss of condition, and damage to teeth. As a result, crib biting in particular has triggered many unkind and ineffectual treatments.

What are they?

In crib biting, the horse grips anything rigid and preferably horizontal with his front teeth, sucks in air, and makes a grunting noise as he does so. If denied, a suitable object to grip, he may learn to use his own knee.

In windsucking, the horse does not grip anything, but arches his neck to take in the air, also making a grunting noise.

It is thought that in both cases the horse creates a vacuum in his throat to gulp down air into his digestive tract, but not all researchers agree with this.

Possible triggers

Crib biting and windsucking are among the most common stereotypies seen in horses. These two behaviors may stem from the horse having been kept short of fibrous feed and the facility to graze at some time in his life, as these behaviors are related to the mouth and digestion.

Many people object to these stereotypies, as they are believed to cause indigestion due to the intake of air to the digestive tract (and, in crib biting, abnormal wear of the front teeth). However, there are reports of horses crib biting when experiencing digestive discomfort, often when the diet is too high in concentrates (grains, pellets, coarse mixes) and low in forage, and of the behavior abating following a change to fewer concentrates and more forage.

My experience is that they do not cause indigestion but result from it, and also from general distress, so there is no need, on practical grounds, to reject such a horse. There is no doubt, though, that constantly hearing or seeing a horse perform them can be irritating, although really you have to feel sorry for them. There is evidence that equine shiatsu therapy can help reduce these problems.

Equally, some horses may have access to ample fibrous feed but start crib biting as a result of overconfinement when denied adequate turnout. Other horses living in the same circumstances, even alongside a crib biter, do not necessarily develop the behavior, confirming that not only does the commencement of a stereotypy depend on individual susceptibility but also that horses do not learn them by copying others.

Fairly recently, it has been discovered that many stabled horses on high concentrate/low fiber rations and with little or no turnout in company have gastric ulcers. The studies were done on racehorses, but it is likely that other horses kept that way are also affected. Ulcers of the digestive system are very painful and highly likely to trigger the development of stereotypies.

What to do

Although it is not known whether either behavior has ever been cured completely, they can often be reduced by giving the horse as stress-free and enjoyable a life as possible. Provide plenty of appealing turnouts with grazing, shelter, and good company.

Pay particular attention to the horse's diet, providing a fairly constant supply of suitable fibrous feed of an energy content that will enable him to eat often enough without becoming fat or bursting with energy. Both hunger and excess energy increase frustration, which in turn leads to the horse performing his stereotypic behavior.

Keep the horse as comfortable as possible. Protect him from insect attacks, use as little clothing as possible since most horses are generally happier without rugs, provide a constant supply of clean water, and give him a clean bed deep enough to encourage him to lie down. Provide him with friendly company, as being alone or with horses he does not like is sure to distress him.

Above right: *Windsucking is done without the horse needing to grip anything such as a fence rail or his stable door.*

Right: *The use of a cribbing collar to keep a horse from crib biting does not always work.*

WHAT *NOT* TO DO

Do not:

- Line your horse's box with barbed or electric wiring to deny him anything to grip.

- Fit him with a cribbing strap—a leather collar with a hard, pointed projection that jabs him in the throat when he arches his neck to suck in air.

- Hit him or yell for performing his stereotypy.

- Fit him with a muzzle.

Weaving

The term "weaving" must have been given to this action when hand looms were widely in use in everyday life, as the horse's side-to-side swaying action is similar to that of a hand-loom weaver.

Below: Antiweaving grills are aimed at keeping the weaver from swinging his head from side to side over his door. However, he may subsequently learn to weave inside his box.

Far left: Feed a weaver first to help him calm down. Making him wait to "teach him to be patient" won't improve matters; horses don't think like that.

WHAT *NOT* TO DO

Do not:

- Fit a weaving grill or full grill to the horse's stable door to prevent him from getting his head over or swinging it from side to side. This will frustrate him even more and he may simply start weaving just behind the grill.

- Suspend bricks or bottles slightly in from each side of the doorway so that he hits his head as he swings from side to side. This is cruel, and the equivalent to hitting him on the head as a punishment. He may associate the unpleasantness or pain with weaving and you might think it would make him stop, but this technique has never cured any weaver.

- Let anyone keep him waiting at feed times to "teach him to wait." This is foolish and will not work. On the contrary, it will make him more anxious than ever and is not conducive to calm eating and good digestion.

What is it?

The horse stands with his head over his stable door and sways from side to side, from one forefoot to the other and back again, his head and neck swinging toward the side on which the foot is on the ground. The forefeet are usually slightly splayed apart and sometimes the foot not bearing weight will actually leave the ground.

Possible triggers

This is a classic sign of worry and frustration at being in a situation the horse feels he can do nothing about. It may therefore be observed at feed times when the horse is waiting to be fed, at the sight of a friend being taken away or coming home, or with the presence of a horse, person, or other animal the affected horse does not like. In addition, when the horse is left alone in the yard or a field, he may weave over the gate because he wants to be taken out or brought in.

Sometimes weaving can occur in transport vehicles when the horse is waiting to be unloaded or otherwise attended to.

What to do

As far as possible, remove all frustrating situations from the horse's life. A common time for weaving to occur is feed time, as the horse can become anxious about waiting to eat, so it is sensible to feed a weaver first to reduce his anxiety at the wait.

If the horse weaves at the proximity of a particular person or animal, try to keep them away from him. This may be difficult, but the reason for the weaving is obvious—and so is the remedy.

If the horse weaves in the absence of his friend, try to give him the opportunity to make other friends and ensure that one of them is nearby for as much of the time as possible.

In short, remove all anxiety-making situations from the horse's life; do not keep him waiting for anything longer than is necessary and, as he is clearly highly strung, feed him a calming diet and make him as comfortable and content as you can.

Nodding and head twirling

Horses do plenty of other things with their heads than the recognized stereotypy of weaving (see pages 86–87). Any strange or abnormal movement of the head is similar to weaving and should be dealt with in a similar manner.

What are they?

The horse will usually stand with his head over the stable door and nod or toss his head up and down, or extend his muzzle and turn and twist his head into various abnormal positions. Often, he will move his top lip around at the same time as he moves his head or flap his lips together (a behavior that can happen in any situation, including under saddle, when the horse is anxious).

Another form of head stereotypy occurs when the horse puts his head over his stable door and scrapes the outside of the door with his teeth in a side-to-side motion, leaving a crescent-shaped mark on the door. As with a crib biter, the edges of the front teeth become abnormally worn—not to mention the door.

Possible triggers

Just like weaving, these behaviors are signs of anxiety, anticipation, and frustration. Waiting for anything, including food, attention, or exercise and turnout, can initiate this behavior. With the exception of door scraping, they often occur when people are nearby and may be at least partly due to the horse seeking attention. He may need or want something specific, or may be extremely bored and desire some kind of company.

These kinds of stereotypies are common at poorly run yards where horses are overconfined and fed too little fiber, kept short of clean water, and/or fed food higher in energy than they need. Lack of visual stimulation is a common cause of such behaviors, as are radios left playing for company. Very few horses really like this background noise, although most will display only small signs of tension in their posture: raised head and neck, bodily tension, an irritated facial expression, ears tense and back or to the side. Others become restless and/or may stop eating. Yet others will move or throw around anything loose in the stable such as buckets, rugs laid over doors, or anything else within reach.

Right: This horse is anxious and distressed. He has thrown his empty net over the door and could well be hungry.

Far right: Head twirling, though often not recognized as such by horse owners, is an abnormal behavior pattern.

What to do

Study your horse thoughtfully with a view to discovering what circumstances cause him to perform his head movements, and then do everything you can to correct the situation.

Generally, remove frustrating factors and give him a life that he finds fulfilling and interesting, which will make him content. Many horses are kept overconfined, given far too little exercise and mind stimulation, and are made uncomfortable with clothing and an inadequate diet.

Because these two behaviors are not generally regarded as official vices, people often regard them with amusement, despite the anxious look in the horse's eyes as he performs them. Subsequently, usually nothing is done to improve the horse's lifestyle. It is often very difficult to persuade people that such a horse has a problem and that he could be helped by more horse-friendly management and care.

There is an argument for adding these behaviors to the list of psychological unsoundnesses that are widely recognized throughout the horse world.

WHAT *NOT* TO DO

Do not:

- Fit a grill of any kind to the top of your horse's stable door to prevent him from performing his head movements.
- Tie him up inside his box "to give him a rest." This is guaranteed to make him want to perform some kind of release behavior even more.
- Fit him with a neck cradle to prevent him from moving his head and neck freely.

Boxwalking

This stereotypy possibly results from past or existing problems based on movement issues—such as overconfinement, being forced to move in stressful ways, or as a reaction to excitement or distress.

What is it?

The most simple, classic form involves the horse walking around and around in his stable, churning a ditch in his bedding and, if it is straw, tangling it up along the way. Some horses appear to be almost in a trance and march around as if in another world, occasionally even knocking over human attendants as if unaware of their presence.

Boxwalking appears to be more common in highly strung and nervous individuals, whatever the breed, but is common in thoroughbreds from racing backgrounds and apparently increases in thoroughbred-type competition breeds that are managed in a similar way. It is more prevalent in young and fit horses in which activity levels are higher than in unfit or older ones, but it continues even when logically the horse should be tired, such as after a hard day's work.

Efforts should certainly be made to modify this behavior because it can be exhausting for the horse, physically and even more so psychologically. If the horse were out, he would move around at least as much as when boxwalking, but it is the lack of mental rest that is so troubling.

Possible triggers

Boxwalking may well have been caused originally by harsh weaning methods in which the foal was taken abruptly from his dam (almost certainly too young, which behavioral researchers now regard as any time before eight months old, as is the usual practice in commercial breeding operations) and stabled with or without company. It may result from overconfinement from an early age even in ethically weaned horses.

Some horses boxwalk at night, possibly out of habit or lack of company and interest. Others boxwalk in anticipation, usually of going to some event, going out for a ride, or just being turned out. Many boxwalkers tramp around in distress when a friend is missing, but don't fully settle even when they are reunited.

An unsuitable diet can also exacerbate or trigger boxwalking. A working horse may need to be fit, so his owner feeds him starch-based concentrates, which can make things worse. High-energy foods can be provided by fibrous foods such as alfalfa, and suit this type of horse better.

WHAT *NOT* TO DO

Do not:
- Tie up your horse to keep him still.
- Sedate or tranquillize him, except on veterinary advice in extreme cases.
- Place obstructions such as straw bales around his track.
- Do anything known to stress the horse.

What to do

Going into the stable and trying to occupy or calm the horse down does not work. Indeed, it appears to add to his frustration. Treatments such as shiatsu may help to calm the behavior for very short periods.

Quiet, stolid companions plus plenty of room to move around—as well as interesting, nonstressful exercise and work—are helpful. Some success has also been achieved by using calming feeds and supplements.

Below: When fence pacing, the horse relentlessly tramps along the fence line. It is similar to boxwalking, but horses don't always do both.

FENCE PACING

This is a version of boxwalking in which the horse walks fast and sometimes trots up and down one particular fence line of the paddock. This may happen regularly or only occasionally, and for either an obvious reason (such as the horse's friend being taken away) or one that is not apparent to us. It may occur even when the horse has his favorite friend with him, and plenty of grass, water, and shelter. In fact, it may seem he has everything he would need to make him happy. Like other stereotypies, once fence pacing has become an established behavior, it seems impossible to cure it completely.

Problems with vet and farrier

A horse known to play up when being treated by a vet or farrier can easily put off potential purchasers. Some farriers will not shoe difficult horses, and they can prove a liability to own.

What happens?

Horses seem to have an innate bad impression where vets and farriers are concerned. It may be their smell (lots of other horses' scents, maybe with equine fear hormones clinging to their clothing), their attitude, the medical smell of vets and, unfortunately, the tough persona of some farriers.

The horse may show the typical signs of suspicion or fear: tension, backing away, raised head, wide eyes, flared nostrils, and snorting. Some begin head tossing, weaving, or pacing. When the dreaded person approaches, some horses actually become violent—rearing, kicking, and biting.

Possible triggers

Nearly always, such a horse has experienced pain or significant discomfort at the hands of a vet or farrier. Injections, wound dressing, and dental work are invariably uncomfortable and often painful. Farriery always involves restricting the horse's precious feet, without which he cannot balance or run away, and it has to be said that some farriers hold up horses' legs for too long and in unnecessarily exaggerated positions. Some are also prone to shouting and exhibit general roughness.

What to do

From very early foalhood, horses should be accustomed gradually, by experienced handlers the foal trusts, to slightly uncomfortable procedures. It often takes two people: one to hold the youngster and one to work. The helper holds the foal gently but with a no-nonsense attitude and plies him with his favorite food, while the other person gradually—maybe over days and weeks—accustoms him to necessary tasks. Associating these tasks with something pleasant means the horse will quickly accept them in the future. On their regular visits, the farrier and vet should pay some attention to the foal, so that they know each other before the foal requires their services.

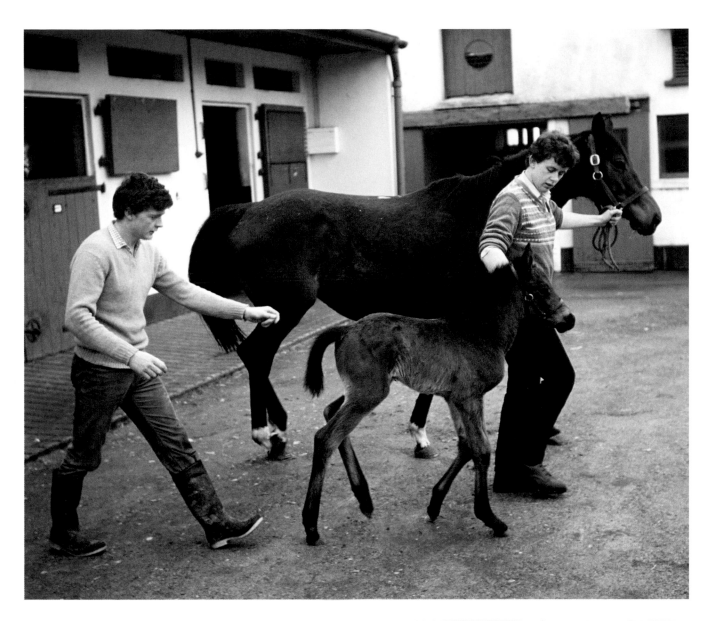

With older, and therefore bigger and stronger horses, a similar routine is advisable. Letting the horse see what is happening and feeding him tasty titbits during the critical moments are often helpful in reassuring and distracting him, and associating the process with pleasure. Some horses, though, accept injections better if their vision is blocked during the process. You also need an understanding and patient vet and farrier if the horse is to develop trust in them.

You can help to retrain your horse by mimicking the shoeing process when you pick out his feet. Hold the leg between your thighs like your farrier does and tap the shoe and hoof wall with a hoof pick, gradually progressing to light and then heavier taps from a hammer, and giving him a food treat only when he cooperates.

Although some experts disagree, others maintain that youngsters can learn by watching older horses having treatment from the vet or farrier—provided the older horses are calm.

USING SEDATION

Vets have a foolproof way of getting a horse to tolerate treatment (which, in many countries, others are not legally allowed to use): sedation by injection. It is probably better to sedate a horse for safety's sake than have him make a habit of objecting to essential treatments, although some say the effect of the sedative prevents the horse from learning to cooperate.

Left: Tapping your horse's hoof firmly with the handle of a hoof pick can simulate nailing on the shoe.

Above: Getting a horse used to visitors from an early age is a great help in getting him to accept vets and farriers.

Frustration

Frustration is experienced by many stabled horses and is the main cause of the development of stereotypies (see pages 82–91) and discontent. Considering the horse's natural life and needs will help you provide solutions.

Above: *Stables with pens outside are much better for horses than buildings where horses are confined indoors.*

Signs of frustration

Just like people, frustration can make a horse feel a range of emotions, from resigned and sad to angry. Some horses show every sign of suffering from depression.

A horse that is suffering from any sort of depressed emotion will be uninterested in his surroundings, lackluster and unenthusiastic, will stand at the back of his box looking miserable, may not eat well, and so on. Anger can result in violence and damage to the stable, or can result in injuries to people and the horse.

Possible triggers

Preventing the horse from doing things he wants and needs to do will cause frustration. Overconfinement is a surefire way to frustrate most horses, particularly in a stable with little mental stimulation. Too much energy and too little liberty, exercise, and work are additional causes. Hunger and thirst are others, as are having to wear clothing, being denied choice, and generally being treated in exactly the opposite way to the natural life horses evolved to lead.

What to do

You can modify your horse's circumstances so that his needs as a horse are met, even though this may be inconvenient for you. Also remember that many horses are quite happy to be in their stables—when they want to be. Few horses want to be out in rain and wind, or in hot sun and when insects make their lives wretched. Consider the following suggestions:

- A well-ventilated stable, as big and high as possible, ideally with more than one view out, and with a deep, clean, dry bed is welcome to almost any horse.
- If your horse can be sure that in his stable he will always find fresh water and several different sources of fiber (hay, haylage, fodder straw, roots, short-chopped forages, and leafy tree branches or twigs to chew on), mimicking the choice he would have in nature, he can come to regard it as a haven.
- As a herd animal, your horse will want his friends close, too. Compatible companions are a natural, ingrained need of horses.
- Create a pen outside the stable so that your horse can come and go as he wishes, rather like having his own private terrace or patio. Even this modest provision greatly reduces the feeling of being shut in. So does the simple measure of putting a chain across the doorway instead of closing the bottom door.
- Try not to use livery yards that do not offer decent, year-round turnout, although not necessarily always on grass. Freedom is really important for happy horses.
- Be willing to lead your horse out to graze as often as possible if turnout is limited at your yard. Rug him up, if appropriate, and enjoy some mutual quiet time.

These basic requirements will keep any horse more content and far less frustrated, providing a domestic version of his birthrights. To treat horses fairly and humanely means allowing them to do horsey things: socializing and mutual grooming with friends, eating suitable feed and moving about for most of their time, lying down to rest away from their own excreta, indulging in the pleasure of rolling, playing around when they want to, breathing clean air, and drinking clean water. These needs are very simple, and will effectively quash feelings of frustration in any horse.

Above: *The marks on these kicking boards show the actions of a frustrated horse who was maybe kicking at a neighbor.*

UNDER SADDLE

To be able to ride is the reason most people buy a horse, but it is when riding that many people start to notice behavioral problems with their horses. Quite a few horses behave differently toward people in the saddle than on the ground. This might be because less competent or experienced people may give their horses no cause for concern on the ground—they don't beat them up or do anything objectionable—but once in the saddle their failings show, often in the form of unintentionally hurting or confusing the horse, and the horse will react accordingly.

Early schooling

Teaching a horse commands and to wear a saddle and bridle is a crucial time in his education. If carried out gradually and skillfully, without confusing or distressing the youngster, he will become trusting and well behaved.

Left: This young horse, on the right, is getting used to wearing and having his halter fitted. It is a good idea to stand him near another, older horse for moral support while learning.

Right: If you sit lightly and don't hassle your horse, he should trot along willingly and with interest.

What is it?

This is the process of getting a horse used to obeying commands, wearing tack and equipment, carrying weight, and learning to associate vocal commands with specific physical movements (called aids) made by the rider's hands, seat, and legs—the object being to enable the horse to be obedient when ridden. It covers the very early months of a horse's schooling.

You may hear the process called "breaking in," "breaking and backing" or, by Western or natural horsemanship trainers,

"starting." To cover all preferences, here it is referred to as "early schooling." This work needs to be done thoroughly, correctly, and carefully, with several months allowed for the horse not only to learn his lessons but also to build up the physical strength needed to carry the weight of a rider.

Possible problems

Horses are often brought into schooling too young (under three years old) and not given the time they need to build up strength during a period when they are still growing. Because horses do not usually mature until six or seven years of age, this can cause problems later, as the horse has not fully understood the vocal commands or physical aids, or been allowed the time for his body to strengthen as well as develop.

When more demanding work is asked for a year or so on, horses often play up out of confusion or even fear, appear to refuse to work, work badly due to tiredness, and may suffer from insidious or more obvious injuries due to overstrain. The answer is always to step back, take expert advice from a vet or behavioral therapist, and remove the pressure.

What to do

If you truly have the skill to give your horse his early schooling yourself, you will be familiar with the techniques, which are covered in any good book on the subject. Try to seek out books and DVDs to help you, ones that claim to use classic principles. These are normally kinder and more time-consuming than harsher methods, but produce excellent results and a happy, confident, and well-developed horse with a good working lifetime in front of him.

If you do not want to school your horse yourself, look for a classic trainer who will visit your horse regularly or take him on their own yard.

Natural horsemanship methods

There are now many trainers who claim to use natural methods for this early schooling. Many of these are based on Western techniques and claim to be quick and humane. With experienced, caring practitioners this can be so, although time is still needed for the horse to develop physical strength.

Possible problems

Some natural horsemanship trainers use methods that involve sending or chasing a horse away from them in a small enclosure until the horse appears to submit. This seems to be effective with domineering horses but can distress more amenable ones, particularly if the trainer misapplies the system by overdoing things and not recognizing the apparent submissiveness of the horse. This treatment is potentially distressing for the animal.

What to do

It can be extremely difficult to know whom to trust with your horse. Contacting official bodies for qualified trainers should result in your finding someone suitable, but not always, so try to also get a recommendation from a horse owner whom you respect. Learn as much as possible so that you can gauge whether or not the advice given to you is accurate or appropriate for you and your horse.

Voice, whip, and body language

These are important tools in schooling horses and must be understood and used correctly to communicate with the horse in a way he understands—without frightening or upsetting him. Instilling obedience to these aids is vital in obtaining control and, therefore, safety. A calm, confident, and patient attitude is also essential.

What are they?

- Your voice is invaluable in training horses, as they are very susceptible to its tone and to associating specific words (sounds, to the horse) with actions. Many people neglect to use the voice. Because it is forbidden in conventional dressage tests, they think it is wrong to use it at other times. When schooling, however, the voice is an extremely valuable aid. Horses really respond to it even though they, as animals, are not particularly vocal.
- Whips vary from long lunging whips to short jumping and racing whips. A horse should not be afraid of a whip. They should be used to give nonpainful touches to encourage the horse, helping him to feel which part of his body the rider wishes him to use, or, from the ground, as a visual guide to where to go. The whip should never be used with force and certainly never as a punishment.
- Body language consists of your posture and actions, which horses watch closely to detect your mood, personality, and intentions. It can also guide them on where to go, either visually from the ground or, through its weight and position, from the saddle.

Possible problems

The main problem with the voice is that many people do not use it enough. Horses actively listen for our voices even though they themselves are not very vocal. A horse can be instantly reassured, calmed, guided, encouraged, corrected, or praised by a familiar sound. As use of the voice is not allowed in conventional competitive dressage, some people mistakenly think it wrong to use it in other situations. Consequently, horses are denied a valuable aid to understanding. On the other hand, babbling incomprehensibly to a horse will simply confuse him.

The problem with whips is that many horses are frightened of the pain they can inflict when used wrongly, ostensibly for punishment, or because the trainer is incapable of self-control. This is, in fact, abuse and a heinous crime in horse training. Pain terrifies and angers horses, and it is understandable if they react violently or uncooperatively to such treatment.

Horses watch us all the time and note every tiny nuance of body language. A horse naturally understands our intentions, mood, and likely actions because body language is his natural way of giving and receiving messages (see pages 26–27). If he gets the wrong message from us because we are careless about what we are saying with our body, he can certainly react in a way we do not want.

What to do

Use your voice quietly to calm, firmly to correct, or brightly to stimulate. Shouting has always been looked down on by good horse people because it frightens many horses. Use the same simple words or phrases for the same purpose every time, perhaps accompanying them with confident, gentle aids from ground or saddle.

Think of the whip as an extension of your hand, used to position a horse, or, visually from the ground, to point to where you want him to go or look. A tap on the root of the tail encourages forward movement; well back on the flank or leg asks him to move away from it; and behind the rider's leg reinforces the leg aid.

Body language should involve a confident, upright, and calm demeanor as the starting, default position. This tells a horse that you are safe to be with, not to be messed about, and not submissive to him. With a nervous horse, let your shoulders slump and allow your head to drop a little to indicate lack of aggression. Unhurried, confident movements reassure a horse. With a horse that is pulling rank and trying to boss you about, square up to him and maybe raise your arms up and toward him. All—except very dominant and possibly aggressive horses—will back down from this posture, and for the exceptions, you should employ a professional to help train them.

If you are employing a teacher or trainer, be extremely careful never to let them be harsh or to actually brutalize your horse by shouting at him or whipping him, and if they expect you to do so, refuse. It may sound strange that a professional trainer would do this but, sadly, some do. As with so many things, a word-of-mouth recommendation is often a good way to find a trainer, but you will know immediately if you feel uncomfortable with someone.

Unfortunately, whips generally have bad connotations. In schooling horses, they are used mainly to reach places you cannot reach yourself. They must certainly never be used to inflict pain on a horse. If you come across a horse who is frightened of a whip, try getting him used to it gradually, by gently stroking him with it, first on his shoulder, while speaking calmly and getting a friend to give him treats at the same time, so that he might come to associate the whip with enjoyment.

Above: Moving toward the rear of your horse can move him on, but facing him from around the front will slow, stop, or turn him.

Left: Gently touching your horse's back leg will stimulate him to move it. If you are calm, your horse will be, too.

Breed temperament

Breeding for temperament has been taken to a fine art by warmblood breeders. The temperament of many warmblood families is now fairly predictable, but is less so in other breeds.

Possible problems

Temperament is a vital quality for many people. Some sellers tell untruths about their horses, so it pays to learn about equine body language in order to trust your own opinion and instinct.

Horses with difficult temperaments are unsuitable for novice owners. Aggressive horses can seriously injure people, and nervous ones can be easily frightened. Then fear overrides all his training and the instinct to flee or fight takes over.

Some breed characteristics

Speaking very generally, the following are the temperament qualities often found in the popular breeds listed. There are individual differences. Remember that ill treatment and poor riding and care can adversely affect any horse's reactions to people, while good management will bring out the best in him.

Thoroughbred Highly strung, sensitive, kind and willing, spirited, they need skilled handling.
Arabian Kind-natured, they like people but don't suffer fools, and are very willing with people they like and trust.
Warmblood Bred to be amenable and placid, and many are (but not all). Stoic, sometimes to their own disadvantage.
Cob Traditionally believed to be very safe, although many aren't. Due to mixed breeding, their temperament is unpredictable. The best look after their riders, and are sensible, kind, and willing.
Native pony Traditionally used as children's mounts, yet many are very strong-minded and need skilled young riders or those who will persevere while learning. Crossbreeds with Arabian blood are often more amenable, if more sensitive.
American saddlebred These are kind, willing, and have an affectionate temperament; often stoic, sensitive, and brave.
Morgan Kind-natured, sometimes quite spirited and full of character. Good for novices and the more expert alike.
Quarter horse Usually placid, amenable, and biddable but not dull or lazy. From working stock, they make good family horses.

Right: Welsh mountain ponies, like this one, are usually kind-natured and patient with very young riders.

Far right: Thoroughbred-type horses need experienced, sensitive, skilled handling, and are usually not suitable for novices.

What to do

When buying a horse, take a professional consultant with you to help you choose an animal that is physically and temperamentally compatible with you, your abilities, and your aims. Ask about the horse's temperament and, although he may behave perfectly for his present owner, watch carefully with your consultant for signs that all may not be as it seems. Often, temperament quirks do not come out until the horse changes homes and is ridden and managed in a different way.

If you do find that your horse's temperament is disappointing or difficult, as long as he is not dangerous, try to work with him and meet him halfway, with professional help. A correct diet that calms him; quiet, firm and positive treatment; and consideration for him as an individual will take you a long way toward success.

Gender issues

Many people have opinions for or against horses of a particular sex. This is often merely a whim with little foundation, yet there are definite differences between the sexes.

Above: Mares' breeding cycles are for the purpose of continuing the species, but some owners object to the temperament changes that occur when their mare is in season.

What are gender issues?

These are the differences in behavior and necessary management associated with horses of the three sexes. In the horse world, there are entire, uncastrated males (stallions), females (mares), and castrated males (geldings). Young entire males under the age of three are called colts, females under the age of three fillies, and the correct word for castration relating to horses is gelding.

Possible problems

Stallions are generally believed to be much more difficult to handle than other horses, but a great deal depends on their owner, rider, and handler. As with any horse, temperament comes into it and many stallions are kind-natured and a pleasure to be around. Stallions usually have pride, sensitivity, and spirit, as well as an eye for the ladies, which means they need firm but kind handling to keep them in line, and few novice owners are capable of providing this. Most stallions can certainly become a liability in the wrong hands.

Accommodation can be difficult, as most livery yards will not accept stallions because they believe they must be turned out alone; they will fight any gelding they see as competition and will want to mate almost any mare in season.

Mares are often underestimated. People forget that they, too, are entire animals and many are more demanding to cope with than a similar gelding. A mare can be moody and difficult when in season, which occurs every three weeks during the warmer months, as her hormones alter her behavior and she is powerless to do anything about it. At this time a mare needs understanding.

Geldings are traditionally regarded as the safest bet for novice owners, but much depends on the individual horse's temperament and life experiences. Many a sweet-natured stallion or mare would be better than an aggressive gelding. Castration stops the production of male hormones and therefore the hormone-related behavior of stallions; however, it is not generally known that about 75 percent of geldings retain some stallion characteristics, although not usually enough to cause problems.

Rigs are males with only one testicle removed. Probably due to a hormonal disorder, which may be inherited, the remaining one is still lodged up inside the abdomen (they normally drop down between the hind legs in a skin bag called the scrotum) producing testosterone, the male hormone. Rigs therefore behave like stallions and often reject other geldings, try to mount mares, and can become aggressive due to frustration and inappropriate handling (usually involving abuse) by unknowledgeable and maybe frightened people.

What to do

Unless you are very knowledgeable and have a firm, calm nature, avoid stallions, as even the best can become dangerous in novice hands.

If a mare's seasons cause problems, discuss the matter with your vet and perhaps try an herb-based feed additive to help her. Make allowances for her during these times, particularly in the spring before her seasons settle down.

Don't think that a gelding will present no problems at all. They are generally the best bet for novice owners but are not robots. Choose your horse for his individual qualities and not solely because he is a gelding. Many geldings retain diluted stallion traits.

Above: Stallions are often chosen for dressage because of their natural inclination to hold themselves proudly and show off.

Lunging

Lunging has been a traditional way of schooling and exercising horses for centuries, and it is excellent if done correctly. If done wrongly, though, it can cause a lot of harm to a horse, including behavioral problems.

What is it?

Lunging is a training method in which the horse wears sturdy headwear, called a "cavesson," from which runs a rein about twenty to thirty feet long to the hand of the trainer, who stands in the middle of a circle, encouraging the horse to move around them. In their other hand the trainer holds a lunging whip about four feet long with a thong roughly twelve feet long, which is used to help control the horse's speed and position.

When beginning lunging, an assistant walks with the horse to keep him out on the circle and help him obey the commands, gradually moving farther away until they are not needed.

Lunging developed because it was a convenient way of asking the horse to move at faster gaits while the trainer could stay in control and did not have to try to keep up with him. Many people keep rigidly to a circle, but this is rather restrictive. It is ideal to ring the changes and walk or run along with your horse on straight lines, then go back to curves.

Possible problems

Circles are unnatural movements for horses; they never perform them at liberty. Because of the changed, exaggerated forces acting on the horse's body, they are quite stressful. The main problems with lunging are:

- Many people make the horse move in too small a circle.
- They also make him go too fast in the belief that they are developing essential free, forward movement.

Small circles increase the stress and are an almost surefire way of causing leg and back injuries. When speed is added, the whole process becomes difficult, harmful, distressing, and even frightening for the horse, as he struggles to keep his feet and counteract the physical discomfort or pain he is feeling.

People often lunge horses for exercise or to get the itch out of their heels before riding. This is fine, provided the horse is properly warmed up in a walk before faster gaits, otherwise he could strain unprepared tissues.

Left: Squeeze with the legs in an on-off way in time with the gait to activate the hind legs and send the horse forward into your contact.

Far left: This young horse is being lunged excellently. He is trotting with classic free, forward movement and no forced posture in a large, loose circle.

Training aids

With young horses, it is best not to use training aids (see pages 110—111) at all but to let the horse get used to working in a free way as naturally as possible. He must be allowed time to develop balance, become stronger and fitter, learn the commands and the whip positions, and generally become confident and cooperative.

When the horse can do all this, we start to develop his riding and weight-bearing muscles. The rider can encourage the correct posture by giving on-off squeezes with her calves in time with the horse's gait. This stimulates his hind legs, bringing them more forward, tucking under his hindquarters, raising his back and belly, and stretching his neck and head out and down. Many people use tight training aids that force his head and neck inward. This causes pain and distress, long-term physical problems, and chronic injuries. These problems can show up as lameness, unnatural movement, and behavioral problems like resistance and defensiveness.

The rider provides a gentle but present contact on the bit which encourages—never forces—the head to come in slightly as the horse finds his balance. If forced beyond the vertical (looking at the horse's face from the side), however, this unnatural posture causes stress and, because of how the horse's eyes work, he will not be able to see where he is going.

A well-proven training aid is the chambon, which, correctly adjusted, only influences the head and neck when the horse holds them too high. Lowering the head and neck naturally lifts the back and encourages the hindquarters to tuck under and the hind legs to reach farther forward, developing the correct posture.

A major error is working the horse for overlong periods. Five minutes is plenty, less for young or unfit horses. Then, any training aid should be released and the horse allowed to fully stretch down his head and neck, also stretching his back. When he has rested, he can work for another short period. For young and unfit horses, twenty minutes of this routine is plenty; for others, up to forty minutes.

What to do

- Only use training aids if absolutely necessary, never with an unfit, green (novice) horse, and only under the supervision of a caring, knowledgeable trainer.
- Lunge for no more than about twenty minutes, giving the horse frequent walk breaks.
- Use large circles in both directions, letting out the whole of the rein except for one loop to allow some leeway should the horse leap around.
- Do not make or allow the horse to go faster than is natural for him unless he is actually lazy and just trudging around. If this persists, have him checked for physical discomfort.

Long-reining

A step up from lunging, long-reining (also known as long-lining) is more versatile; it can train a horse up to high school level, teaches him to accept a bit, and fully prepares him for being ridden. Done well, long-reining develops the horse's confidence, trust, and cooperation, which makes for obedience.

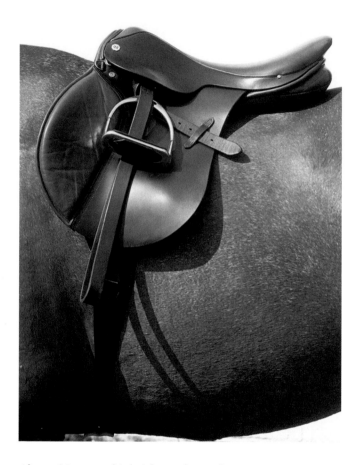

Above: Stirrups at this height can be used for an experienced horse. For a youngster, have them down and tied together under his breastbone.

Right: When using longreins, they should be safely held up by being passed through the rings on the roller, and the handler should not hang on the horse's mouth.

What is it?

In long-reining, two lunging reins are used, clipped to the side rings of a cavesson or the bit rings of a bridle. They pass back, one rein on each side of the horse, through the stirrups on a saddle or the rings on a training roller. If a saddle is used, the stirrups must be tied together under the horse's girth area to keep them from swinging around.

The trainer takes one rein in each hand and walks behind the horse, guiding him with voice, gentle feels on the bit, the feel of the rein on his side, and an occasional tap with the long whip if necessary. The trainer walks or runs mainly behind the horse or, as required, to one side roughly level with his hip. The distance at which the trainer walks behind the horse can vary, so long as the trainer feels safe and in control.

Horses generally take well to long-reining. They should be good at lunging before progressing to long reins.

Possible problems

The trainer needs to be fitter and more agile than for lunging in order to keep up with the horse at walk and trot. Otherwise, the trainer may allow the horse to pull them along, which will hurt the horse's mouth and have a negative effect on his training. Another problem is that of handling two reins and the whip.

From the horse's viewpoint, he may object to feeling reins in unfamiliar places and may kick out or otherwise play up.

What to do

You have to get fit for long-reining, although you can do so while you practice. Start by using a cavesson, not a bit, in case you find yourself being pulled along. Begin at a walk in an safe, enclosed area and gradually build up to running with the horse. As you get fitter, the horse becomes more practiced, and as you get better at handling the reins and whip, you can long-rein around the stable premises and also outside. Do not hesitate to recruit an assistant to walk at your horse's head or lead him, especially if you are going out and about. You cannot take too many safety precautions.

When fitting the reins, first rub them up and down the horse's legs and on his sides. Also let him feel them across his back until he is completely unfazed by them. Have a helper holding him and giving him tidbits while you do this. By leading him at first, your helper can accustom the horse to working, no longer on circles or large ovals as on the lunge, but leading the way and potentially working anywhere.

Use your voice aids often and clearly, and if there is any chance he might not obey, have a helper at his head and do not take him out in public places.

Most horses really seem to enjoy long-reining. It teaches them to listen to the trainer and the reins, and develops their initiative and confidence.

NAPPING AND PLANTING

Long-reining a horse with a rider on board is an excellent remedy for horses who have started napping (refusing to go forward but possibly moving sideways or backward) or planting (rooting to the spot). The instant the horse naps, the rider applies firm leg aids and tells the horse sharply to walk on while the trainer walking behind taps him on the quarters with the whip and shakes the reins along his sides. Few horses resist this dual effect for long.

The variety of tack and training aids now available can be really confusing, and the best advice is to keep it simple. It is important to choose good-quality equipment for safety and durability, and to use no more than your horse really needs. Badly fitted and adjusted tack causes chronic injuries, as well as many problem behaviors in horses as they try to escape the discomfort and pain they are feeling.

Tack and training aids

SADDLES

The most important points about a saddle are:

- It must be suitable for your type of riding.
- It must be comfortable for you and your horse.

There are traditional saddles made from leather on beechwood trees (frames) with the panels beneath the seat stuffed with wool. There are also entirely synthetic saddles, saddles with air-filled panels, saddles without trees, and saddles with adjustable gullets. Some saddles also flex with the horse.

There are saddles for every discipline, but for general riding try a general-purpose, working hunter or VSD (very slightly dressage), which gives more knee room at the front of the flap than a pure dressage saddle.

Whatever type of saddle you have, reread the points about fit and maintenance on pages 52–53.

Saddles can be expensive, so it is worth registering them with a security provider to be microchipped or marked with a code. Many livery owners take their saddles home, as livery yards and riding schools are regularly targeted by thieves.

BRIDLES AND BITS

Again, quality and comfort are key. Saddle fit and adjustment are covered on pages 52–53.

Generally, the mildest bit that gives you control and gives your horse comfort is what you should use. Your riding should certainly not depend mainly on your bit, but you must have a bit your horse respects.

Many horses that appear to have problems accepting a bit go well in bitless bridles. Some have awkwardly conformed mouths that make fitting a comfortable bit difficult, and these are good candidates for trying a bitless bridle. Memories of pain from a bit can cause riding difficulties in some horses, so in these cases it is also worth trying a bitless bridle.

Some bitless bridles, with a long shank hanging down from the side of the noseband, work on a leverage principle and can be very powerful, putting pressure on the horse's nose, jaw, and poll. Milder ones have the reins attached directly to the side of the noseband, or form a loop or cross pattern under the horse's jaw. With expert supervision, try to work with various types to see which suits your horse best.

TRAINING AIDS

Training aids should be used rarely and temporarily to help a horse understand the posture in which he needs to work in order to carry weight safely, and, as he strengthens up, more comfortably and effectively. If a horse carries his head too high, pokes his nose too much, trails his hind legs, and so on, a training aid can gently persuade him into, and thereby give him the feel of, a correct posture. Training aids were never intended to coerce the horse into an exaggerated posture with his neck shortened, his face well behind the vertical, or even with his chin on his chest (which is extremely distressing and injurious) or bundled up to the extent that he cannot move freely and use and develop his muscles properly.

Problems arise when people use them wrongly to create forced, exaggerated postures. Do not use any item that is actually designed to bring the horse's nose in toward his chest, because this posture can be damaging to his body and mind. Also, never leave your horse strapped down like this in the stable or tied up, no matter who advises it or for whatever plausible-sounding reason. The proven, correct, humane training and working posture is for the horse to have the front of his face in front of a vertical line dropped from his forehead to the ground.

Used properly, training aids can play a useful role in schooling and developing horses. Used wrongly, they can cause long-term damage to a horse's mind and body, which can only be termed abuse.

Above: *A well-placed saddle, well-fitting tack, and protected legs all contribute toward the comfort of the horse when being ridden.*

Left: *Wearing a running martingale will keep the reins still and in place. Along with a well-fitting bit, this helps make for a comfortable horse.*

Bitting problems

Bits have long been a cause of much fascination for some people, if not their horses. The right bit can make a massive difference to a horse, but they are not magic solutions to behavior and training difficulties. It is a combination of the right bit and sensitive, educated hands that makes a horse happy in his mouth.

Above: A cheeked snaffle bit helps a young or green horse keep the bit central in the mouth should he throw his head around.

Right: There are many different bits available to suit the mouth shapes and preferences of different horses. A small selection is shown here.

What is it?

Bitting is the name given to the subject of understanding horse bits: how they are made, how the different designs work, how they should fit and be used, and the effects they should have on the horse.

Possible problems

Problems in getting a horse to accept the bit are not uncommon, and this is hardly surprising. Anyone who wears dentures knows how unpleasant they are and what it takes to get used to them—and we have a choice. The horse does not, and is usually made to wear a bit his owner or rider thinks is best for him, whether it actually is or not.

Horses with bitting problems always show it, and it is up to us to solve them. We need to have the humility to admit that our choice may not be right for the horse and, even more importantly, that we may be using the bit wrongly.

Signs of bitting problems include:

- The horse salivating excessively, maybe drooling, which indicates distress and even pain. Contrary to popular opinion, a horse's mouth should be just moist and no more.
- Head tossing.
- A distressed, frightened, angry, or locked-down expression about the horse's head and face.
- Nostrils flared and wrinkled back, lips tense and maybe too mobile.
- Uneven gaits, poor rhythm, and crookedness.
- The horse on a loose rein carrying his head behind the vertical, trying to escape the bit.
- The horse sweating from distress and the effort of combating harsh riding.

What to do

You will probably need professional help to rethink what sort of bit your horse should have. Get your horse's mouth and teeth checked (see pages 42–43). Make sure that the bit you choose is a comfortable shape for his mouth, and remember that bitting theories often do not work for every horse. Then check that the bit you have chosen is positioned correctly (see pages 52–53).

- Single-jointed snaffles are extremely common and not a horse-friendly shape—no horse has a V-shaped mouth. French-link snaffles mold more considerately to the shape of the mouth.
- Straight-bar mouthpieces are uncomfortable and allow no room for the tongue.
- Ported mouthpieces are often uncomfortable, as the angles at the ends of the port often come right on the bars of the horse's mouth—the gap between the front and back teeth where the bit rests, which is thinly covered with skin and is

very sensitive. High ports can press painfully into the roof of the horse's mouth. Half-moon (also called mullen) mouthpieces, though, are simple and leave enough room for the tongue.
- Curb chains should be smooth and fit right down into the curb/chin groove, not ride up the jaw and rub the thin skin there.
- Don't fall for the hype about flavored bits. Your horse may hate them. Go for unflavored materials and give your horse a mint when tacking up.

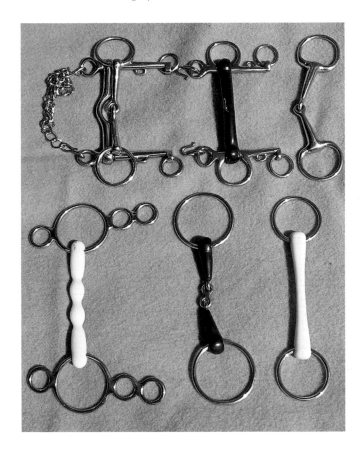

NAPPING AND PLANTING BIT CONTACT

An acceptable contact on a snaffle is the same as a comfortable handshake, enough to take a toddler for a walk or hold a bird to restrain but not hurt it—and much less on a curb.

Lack of cooperation

Horses nearly always get the blame when they aren't cooperating. As a species, they are such laid-back, amenable creatures that we should realize that willful disobedience is unlikely to be the reason.

What is it?

Lack of cooperation takes many forms. Basically, the horse will simply not work the way we think he should. He may play up mildly or violently, shy at apparently nothing (as what many people term an excuse not to work), refuse or run out at jumps, or deliberately ignore the rider's aids, and several other antics as well. Before accusing your horse of disobedience and calling him names, you should take a step back and think about what could be wrong.

Possible triggers

There is the simple reason that the horse may just not feel like working (we all know how that feels)—and how do we know whether or not, for example, he has a headache, is a little sore somewhere, or is not feeling very well?

Other things to think about are definite discomfort or pain somewhere in the horse's body. The parts that easily cause trouble are the mouth, teeth, back, and feet. If your horse is separated from a close friend during his work, this is may also affect his behavior. We should also remember that horses, like us, get on with some people but not others, so there is the chance that he has no confidence in whoever is handling or riding him at that moment.

Finally, there is the one cause you probably don't want to think about: the possibility that your style of riding is upsetting or stressing him and he just can't take it.

What to do

- Check your horse's vital health signs first to see if he could be unwell (see pages 48–49). He should also have bright eyes, mobile ears, an interested expression, and no tension in his muscles.
- To check for pain in the foot or lower leg, feel for your horse's digital pulse immediately above the fetlock on the side of the leg. If it is strong or pounding, he is in pain—although he could be in discomfort even if it isn't. Check for a stone bruising his foot or a problem with his shoe.
- Check that his urine and droppings are normal.
- Check your horse's body for wounds, lumps, bumps, new swellings, or sore patches.
- Check the fit and comfort of his saddle, bridle, bit, and rugs. If you are unsure, consult a saddle fitter. Check particularly the head, withers, back, and whole girth area for tack injuries, including bare, swollen, or raw patches.
- Watch your horse's demeanor with and without his bit and when he eats, to detect possible mouth injuries. Are his eating and drinking behavior normal?

ASK YOURSELF

Some horses appear to be uncooperative when in fact they just cannot tolerate the way they are being ridden. If you know you have riding faults, or if a good teacher has repeatedly told you that you have such faults, don't make the excuse that that's just the way you ride. For the well-being of your horse and your own clear conscience, you need to take effective steps to remedy the situation.

Left: Refusals are nearly always rider error, due to not presenting the horse correctly or not ensuring that he is well and experienced enough to tackle the obstacle.

Right: Horses who behave like this may have a good reason, but they are not suitable for novice handlers.

Napping, rearing, and running back

These three problem behaviors are all related and can be very dangerous. They used to be thought of as disobedience but are now more often regarded as being due to fear. Horses easily develop habits associated with particular places or even people, so these fears need to be overcome quickly.

Above: *If a horse starts to rear, he may or may not go right up. The rider should concentrate on getting quick, forward movement to avoid a full rear.*

Right: *This horse is going into a full rear and the rider is exerting downward pressure on the bit. She should release it and give strong forward leg aids instead.*

What are they?

These behaviors are all refusals of the horse to go forward and to work.

Napping (also called balking or jibbing) is when a horse refuses to go forward. The rider can use as strong aids as they like, but this usually does not work and often makes things worse.

Rearing is when the horse stands up on his hind legs. It is extremely dangerous, as the horse can easily fall over on top of his rider, with serious or even fatal results.

Running backward develops from napping and is dangerous because the horse can run into risky situations or objects, such as down ditches or into piles of rubble, vehicles, people, or buildings, and can also fall down as he loses his balance.

Possible triggers

Horses have often been whipped for these perceived rebellions, but behavioral scientists now believe that such problems are mostly caused by:

- Fear of going on because of what is ahead.
- Concern about being ridden or driven due to associated discomfort, pain, effort, or fatigue.
- The horse not feeling strong or well enough to work.
- A habit; for example, when a horse always naps at the same place.

What to do

With all three problems, giving the horse a lead from another that will proceed calmly and without hesitation usually works. With this technique, you are using the herd instinct to your advantage. Over time, the two horses can be ridden progressively farther apart until company is no longer needed.

As the horse is usually worried, it compounds the problem if you hit him, confirming that there is something to fear. The fact that he will proceed with another horse but not with a human shows where his confidence lies, so your relationship is not strong enough. If you can always be a strong leader type who never hurts or frightens your horse, in time he should come to feel safe with you and go where you ask. Dismounting to lead him usually works, as he can follow you and, in time, this becomes unnecessary.

If you are caught on your own and do not want to dismount, circling and riding backward and forward nearer to the stopping point will usually work in the end, but may take some considerable time and requires calm persistence and utter commitment on your part.

Napping See long-reining on pages 108–109.

Rearing Sit upright and still, with no pressure on the horse's mouth. If you unbalance your horse and he falls, you could be severly injured. Command him to walk on; the instant his forefeet touch the ground, send him forward with your legs

and the "walk on" command, in any direction so long as you keep him walking, and praise him for doing so. Rearers are often frightened of the bit and/or the way the rider uses their hands, so check these aspects carefully (see pages 112–113).

Running backward Try to turn the horse around using strong aids, as this nearly always stops his progress. Walk him around purposefully and calmly near his stopping point, turning him again if he goes backward, and in time he will move forward.

Horses confirmed in these three practices need sensitive and firm reschooling by an expert handler who will not brutalize them but will concentrate on training in instant and infallible forward movement, as all three practices stem from backward thinking on the part of the horse. Various brutal remedies have been suggested over the generations, but with our modern understanding of the horse's mind, it should be possible to retrain horses effectively and humanely.

Bucking

A determined bucker has found a surefire way of getting rid of his rider—even a rodeo rider will fall off eventually. But how do you stop such a horse from carrying out this behavior?

What is it?

Bucking comprises minor or major leaps in the air, sometimes off all four feet with the horse's back arched and his head between his knees, or sometimes with the horse lifting his hindquarters, and perhaps kicking out while in the air. As he moves along, he will land alternately on his hindfeet and forefeet, and repeat the process.

Possible triggers

Back and saddle problems are common causes. Pain or discomfort in the saddle and girth areas can cause a horse to buck in objection.

Some horses buck because they learned that it gets rid of riders. Even if a horse is pain-free and well ridden, he may still associate being ridden with past pain experienced, bad riding, hard work, and a stressful time. Bucking to unseat the rider is a way of objecting that comes naturally to the horse.

RIDING A BUCKER

Most horses need to get their heads down in order to buck seriously, although small bucks can be performed with the head up.

Ride a bucker in a humane bit that he respects enough not to push his head down. Be careful when giving a bucker rests on a long rein, doing so only when at a halt or walk.

If, at other gaits, you maintain a reasonable contact and keep his head up, bucking is unlikely. If he does buck, sit up, get his head up, and kick on forward—crude but effective: safety is what matters. When the bucking stops, ride on normally, keeping his head up.

Do not whip the horse, as this is almost guaranteed to make the bucking worse.

Right: This rider is doing a great job of staying in the saddle.

Far right: When an unridden horse bucks, it can be a sign of enjoying his freedom.

What to do

Check the horse's back and girth area for discomfort or pain. Look for sore muscles, a bruise from rolling on a stone, sore skin from a saddle rub, dirt or debris between the saddle (or pad) and the horse, an insect bite, girth galls (sore or raw patches), bruising behind the elbows because the girth comes too far forward, and so on.

Get your saddle and girth checked by a qualified saddle fitter. Uneven pressure from the saddle due to lumpy, uneven, or inadequate stuffing, a damaged saddle tree, poor fit, or friction can all cause discomfort and pain.

A rider with an unbalanced, uneven seat in the saddle who moves around too much, bangs heavily into the saddle, and so on can annoy the horse and actually cause injury, as the horse uses unaccustomed muscles to cope with his erratic load and still do as he is asked.

All healthy, normal horses possess a buck that can unseat any rider, if they wish. Think of rodeo riders; they nearly all come off eventually. Bucking needs serious attention, as it is potentially dangerous.

IN THE FIELD

Although we have little control over horses when they are turned out, there are ways of managing them to avoid the behavioral problems that can cause injury or unrest. While injuries do occur in the field, they also occur during work, around the stable yard, and in the stable. Therefore, possible injuries are no reason to deny a horse the freedom he needs to remain healthy and happy.

Turnout does not have to be on grass. Surfaced areas with hay and water are good for horses that require limited grazing or when the land is unsuitable for turning out.

Horses are social animals by nature and need the company of their own kind. A natural, mixed herd structure should guide you when planning domestic turnout arrangements, as this will encourage contentment and peace.

Segregation

WHAT IS IT?

Segregation is the practice of separating horses, usually into sex and/or age groups, for their time in the field and sometimes even in the stable yard. In nature, segregation of that kind does not happen except with "bachelor bands"—groups of males that are either too young or too old to have herds of their own and who have left or been kicked out of a herd with a (possibly new) reigning stallion.

WHY IS IT PRACTICED?

Some yard owners feel that it is not safe to graze mares and geldings together because they believe that there will be skirmishes and frequent injuries.

On studs, young stock are invariably segregated according to sex if the males are still entire, as otherwise there would be arguments among the colts and possibly injuries, and probable pregnancies in the older fillies.

An umbrella reason for segregating horses is to avoid injury. This is understandable, but we cannot wrap our horses in blankets and there are limits to what horses should have to put up with. Anything to do with horses is risky, but trying unreasonably to avoid the risk is often unfair to those horses.

PROBLEMS WITH SEGREGATION

Over the last ten or fifteen years, segregating horses by sex has become relatively common. It seems to be almost a standard practice that is adhered to rigidly and quite unreasonably in some yards. This may be because those who do it have not really thought through the situation, because in fact it is not only unnecessary but can be unfair to the horses.

If a mare and gelding are close friends—and many are—it is really unkind to separate them during their turnout time, particularly if they are not stabled near each other or worked together. This is poor horse care and can affect the horses' well-being, both physically and mentally. There is absolutely no guarantee that same-sex groups will contain compatible animals or be happier or safer than mixed-sex ones, and a more understanding and caring attitude should be adopted.

Even worse is the common practice of segregating horses by turning them out in small, individual paddocks separated by electric fencing, so that they cannot mutually groom each other, as they dare not go near the fence. This denies the animals one of the "Five Freedoms" of animal welfare (see pages 22–23), which states that horses must be

allowed to express most patterns of normal behavior, with company of the animal's own kind. This is an innate need.

On studs, placing young animals in same-sex groups without an older mare and/or gelding with them leads to the youngsters not learning natural herd manners at a time when they are growing up and in need of adult discipline and guidance. This constitutes an abnormal upbringing and is not in the best interests of the animals. Peer groups (same age and, usually, sex) do not give horses normal equine mores, and such horses are, later, often more difficult for people to train.

WHAT TO DO

The important criterion is that nonbreeding horses should be allowed their liberty with whichever animals they get along with—their friends—regardless of whether they are mares or geldings. They should not be separated from their preferred companions and segregated into same-sex groups, which may easily contain incompatible horses that are unfriendly toward each other.

Watch the horses in your yard carefully so you know who is friendly with whom, then always try to turn those horses out together, for their sakes and so that peace reigns.

Above: *Friends grazing at dawn. A peaceful life with their friends and family is dear to the hearts of all horses.*

Left: *Mares and foals in neighboring fields—together, yet apart—will probably be quite happy.*

Company, right and wrong

Horses are social herd animals and nearly all of them need company of their own kind if they are to thrive, but that company has to be suitable or there could be serious problems.

Effects of company

If horses are mixed with the wrong sort of company, whether in the stable yard, when at liberty with each other, or while working, it can create conflict (see pages 126–127). This conflict may result in psychological distress or injuries to the horses concerned.

When horses are mixed with the right sort of company, they will be seen to thrive, injuries are far fewer (although horseplay is often rough), and the horses are mentally well-balanced and easier for people to deal with.

The fact that in a feral herd horses have to live with a situation is no reason for enforcing it on domestic horses. Surely one of the advantages of domestication is that we can make lives more pleasant and healthy for our horses in exchange for their work and company. Nature is a good guide, but she doesn't have all the answers.

The right company

Good company is any other horse with which your horse gets along well. This does not necessarily mean that the companion (or companions) will be the same sex or even the same age.

Observe the horses yours mixes with and watch to see which ones seem to be his friends, which ones he does not bother with, and which seem to not be friends (or are even enemies). Friends will usually spend most of their time with, or near, each other. They may graze closely, groom each other, play together, stand in the shade together, go to drink at the same time, and so on. There is rarely any tension or argument between them. For their contentment, they should be stabled close to each other and turned out together. If they are not, you may notice signs of distress when they are separated, which will last usually only until the companion returns (see pages 72–73).

Left: *An interesting situation. Clearly there are two pairs of friends who graze with each other but not together, showing that horses do play favorites.*

Below: *From the postures and expressions of these horses, it is clear that they are friends indulging in horseplay and having fun.*

The wrong company

The wrong company is any horse with which yours does not get along. A horse that drives yours around the field, constantly moving him on, denying him his favored company, keeping him away from water and shelter, or even bullying and fighting him, is certainly the wrong company.

In nature, horses have space to escape from a horse they do not like or which is harassing or bullying them, but in a domestic field this is more difficult. It is particularly stressful for your horse to be stabled next to—or even within sight or earshot of—a dominant, aggressive, bullying horse because such proximity is distressing and there is no escape.

What to do

In large yards, arrange for friends to be stabled near each other and turned out together. It is good management to keep apart those that do not get along, because the proximity of an unfriendly horse is stressful for both parties and will eventually affect their health. The adrenaline will keep flowing and both will be more or less on alert all the time, with their fight-or-flight instincts permanently switched on. This is physically and mentally exhausting.

Conversely, mixing compatible horses together away from incompatible ones makes for happiness, contentment, and a feeling of security and companionship that actively promotes good psychological and physical well-being. The mind definitely affects the body, for better or worse.

Although we humans have to learn to tolerate other people, even if we don't get along, horses' minds do not work in the same way and they have no understanding of this. As a result, keeping enemies together to teach them to get along simply will not work.

Conflict

Although horses are largely peaceful animals, occasionally herd politics rears its head and arguments occur. Horses fight and play rough, and steps must be taken to avoid injury.

What is it?

Conflict can mean any ill feeling between horses, but particularly when physical contact occurs during minor scuffles or major fighting. As explained on pages 124–125, living in a heightened state of defense or aggression is bad for the horses' health, but actual fighting among them can result in serious physical injuries.

Possible triggers

In domestic circumstances, overcrowding is a major cause of conflict. Horses can feel ambivalent toward others, and when crowded together in the field or in working situations, a skirmish can easily break out.

Friendship rivalries occasionally cause problems. Horses have what scientists call preferred associates—"friends" to you and me—and normally form close pair bonds. This is quite natural and to be expected. Problems can arise when a third horse

wants to be included. Sometimes this is permitted but occasionally jealousy arises and conflict occurs between the newcomer and one of the others.

Conflict over food is also common. Such resources are important to horses and arguments can break out when food is scarce, such as when limited piles of hay are set out for a large group of horses. Shelter can be another important resource to many horses, so conflict may arise over access to the best shade tree in summer or the field shelter in winter.

In feral situations, conflict is normal and natural among rival stallions. Sexually mature males are often ejected from the herd by the stallion if they repeatedly show interest in the mares. A strange stallion, maybe from a bachelor band or a youngster from another herd, that is looking to come in and take over will also stimulate conflict. This is at the root of domestic horseplay, even though the situation may not have a sexual basis.

What to do

When horses are loose together, there is not a lot you can do to resolve conflict without putting yourself in danger. If the horses and people know each other well and the humans have an authoritative, mutually trusting relationship with the horses, they may be able to go into the area to stop an argument or even a fight. A stern voice and confident posture are needed. A hose and buckets of water can also be used effectively to break up serious fights!

This can be a dangerous situation. Skilled, knowledgeable professionals may attempt it, but it is not for most of us. It is much more effective and safer to prevent conflict in the first place.

• Introduce new horses to a herd or yard gradually, under human supervision. First ride the newcomer with a horse-friendly herd member. Turn them out in neighboring fields with high, secure fencing between them, then introduce one more herd member at a time, or some similar procedure.

• Keep in-season females away from colts and stallions unless breeding.

• Keep known adversaries apart in stables and paddocks, and try not to ride them near each other during work.

Above: *Wild stallion tactics can be vicious. They try to trip up their opponents, then they go for the soft flanks to disembowel them.*

Left: *In a large paddock, there is often room for a horse to run away from an aggressive companion, but if such behavior happens regularly, the horses should be separated.*

Rolling

Horses enjoy rolling tremendously, and people enjoy watching them do it, too. Everything should be done to allow and encourage horses to roll, but not when they're working.

What is it?

When a horse wants to roll, he will drop his head to smell out a suitable place. He will probably paw the ground, then fold his knees, go down forehand-first, flop over on one side, then roll around on his side and back. Some horses do one side, then get up, go down again, and do the other side. It is said to be a sign of health and agility if a horse can roll over from one side to the other without having to get up in between.

Why do horses do it?

Rolling may be a form of self-massage. It is almost certainly a natural form of coat and skin care. Dried-on mud, for example, gives some protection against wind, and dust and earth in the coat may repel skin parasites. Horses often have set rolling places and line up to use them. It is possible that the combined scents of the individual horses make up a herd smell, which they all want to cover themselves with to confirm acceptance in their herd.

Horses also roll when they are hot and sweaty or after they have been given a bath. Horses often want to roll on soft ground and even in water with a soft base, such as the sea on a sandy shore.

Encouraging rolling

To encourage horses to roll, they must be turned out on ground that is inviting to them—grass, earth, or mud, or a surfaced area such as an arena. If horses are mainly stabled and are not being turned out, a sand bath or some other soft area should be created for them and they should be taken there daily to roll in hand. When holding a horse on a lead rope that is rolling, stand at his head facing him when he is down. This keeps you safe and out of the way of his legs and feet as he rolls.

If you are on soft ground such as sand or in water with a soft base, your horse may start to go down to roll, regardless of rider and tack. This can be quite dangerous, and at least risks

damage to the saddle tree. If your horse drops his head and starts to sniff or paw, suggesting he is about to go down, get his head up at once and move him on with firm leg aids. If his knees start to buckle and he is going down, you are probably at the point of no return, although quick action even then might save the day—and save you a soaking. If you're too late, quit your stirrups and jump off, and get out of harm's way.

Many people fence off areas of water such as ponds in their horses' fields, which is a great shame. Provided they have a safe approach and footing, they can be left to provide an extra pleasure facility for domestic horses, whose environments are often very restricted. Care must be taken over ditches, though, and it is usually safest to fence them off. Horses can roll or lie down near ditches and fall into them, becoming stuck. Many a horse has lost its life because of this.

HEALTH TIP

When horses get up from rolling, they almost always have a good shake, which is a sign of well-being. If a horse rolls without then shaking, it can be a sign of abdominal discomfort or pain, such as colic, and you should watch him closely for a repetition of this and other signs of poor health.

Left: Shaking after rolling loosens the dust and debris picked up, and makes the horse feel good.

Far left: Horses may roll for fun or because they are suffering from colic. If the latter, other signs of pain will be present.

Play

As in other species, play is a way for young horses to learn about relationships, for their future lives. But adult animals play, too, and they obviously enjoy themselves.

Above: *These two Friesians work and play together. They are clearly delighted in each other's company.*

Right: *Horseplay starts at a young age in preparation for adult life. Foals that are not allowed to play with others can develop psychological disorders and lack of sociability.*

What is it?

When playing, horses will run about with each other, usually in pairs. They perform all sorts of antics: leaps into the air, biting and pushing each other, pretending to kick by raising their hindquarters but not kicking out, standing on their hind legs and "boxing," squealing, snorting, and generally getting quite rough with each other.

It is noticeable that other horses normally keep away from a pair that are playing, although they may watch them and perhaps run around them a few feet away, looking like referees, although they rarely interfere.

Sometimes a whole group of horses or ponies will charge around together, clearly enjoying this communal run. In these cases, there will be less acrobatics than are seen in pair play.

Possible problems

Horses rarely sustain significant injuries when playing. They hardly ever hurt each other and seem to know just how far to go with a playmate.

Occasionally—and usually in horses that are generally deprived of the opportunity to play—they may go on for rather a long time very energetically and start to become overly excited, sweaty (particularly if they are rugged), and tired. If it is a cold and windy winter's day, the horses can then become chilled when the play stops and they stand around, although those that are rugged may be at an advantage and they will probably come to no harm, particularly if the field has good shelter. The best solution is, of course, to turn out horses regularly so that it does not become such an exciting treat.

People often worry about shod horses playing with each other, as an accidental kick from a steel-shod hoof can easily break a bone. Such accidents do happen, but they are rare.

How to make play safer

Play is an important social and psychological activity for horses, as it is for other animals, much like children. It enables them to let off steam, exercise themselves and test their bodies, develops balance and judgment, tests and strengthens relationships, and gives pleasure. To make it as safe as is reasonably possible, you should consider the following precautions:

• Turn out only compatible horses together.
• Make sure the ground surface and fencing are safe—not stony or strewn with litter or equipment that has not been put away, no barbed wire or loose fencing, nor protrusions in the field such as loose fence posts. Troughs set at an angle to the fence should have rails running from their ends to the fence to even off the obstruction they can cause to galloping horses.
• Turn out horses every day if possible, so that they do not become crazy with excitement when they do go out.
• Put protective boots on their legs, such as brushing or tendon boots.
• Turn out horses slightly hungry, so that they will be busy looking for tasty grass, which has a lethargic effect on horses in any case.

Personal space

Most animals and humans are particular about whom they like to have near them, and horses are no different. However, their space preferences are stronger and much more extensive than those of most of us.

What is it?

Behavioral researchers and other experienced horse watchers have observed that horses seem to create around them an oval shape (with invisible barriers, of course) roughly twenty-five feet away from their bodies. The idea is that they only allow those they like or trust to cross those barriers and come closer to them.

Horses are prey animals, so it is reasonable for them to be aware of their own space, because if a predator comes too close they stand a good chance of being killed. Through the study of zebras and lions, it is suggested that the personal space horses designate for predators is around seventy-five feet. This appears to be the safe distance to which a predator can approach that still allows the horse—an expert at explosive standing starts—a good chance of escaping with his life.

Possible problems

If you have the chance to observe young foals that have not been handled much, you will soon learn about their personal space. Although they take their cues from their dams, who will probably allow humans full-on contact, the foals usually do not and hover warily a little distance away.

It is usually safest to enter a field of horses you do not know only with someone who does know them, because not all of the horses may welcome visitors. Some will move away from an unfamiliar person, whereas others will allow you to approach. If unhappy with your presence, some might even enter your space and make threatening gestures or even attack you—and a single human is no match for such a horse. If you find yourself in trouble, an upright, confident posture helps.

Below: A quality arrangement of paddocks. The double fencing keeps neighbors well away from each other.

Below: It is wise to stand back from an unfamiliar horse and use your voice when approaching him, letting him smell you as you get closer.

Crowding too many horses into too small an area can also create problems with personal space limits and, therefore, relationships. For example, if you have to use an arena as turnout when the pasture is unsuitable (too wet, too hard), you will probably find that two friendly horses in an area of 120 feet by 60 feet is enough. Turning out horses that do not get along in such a small area would be asking for serious trouble.

Other considerations

Domestic horses obviously allow people into their space because they have usually been accustomed to being handled since an early age. Few people ask a horse if they can approach him, although the more experienced and sensitive do. It is a polite and safe practice to approach a strange horse and stand back a little, talking to him and letting him smell you, rather than going straight up to him. Do not take tidbits into a field unless you are prepared to be mobbed.

When lunging a horse, some people bring the horse to them in the center of the circle for a tidbit or to change the rein (direction). This amounts to letting the horse enter your space, which may not be a good idea with a strong-minded type. By standing him out on the circle and approaching him, you are invading his space, which is a dominant action and puts you in charge.

When riding with a new companion, you can control your horses' reactions, and this can be a good way of introducing them. Only really undisciplined horses will pick a fight under saddle, although stallions may try to mount mares in season if not taught self-control.

Reluctance to lie down

Although horses can sleep lightly standing up, they need to lie down to sleep deeply and fully refresh themselves. However, lying down and getting up is quite hard work for a horse.

Above: Horses lie down and get up with their front legs first. Horses' legs are delicate, so both processes are hard work.

Right: The natural instinct of feral horses to not lie down all at the same time can still be seen in large domestic herds.

How does he do it?

Horses lie down by folding their knees and flopping onto one side. To lie flat out, they let themselves go completely and stretch out. To get up, a horse must first raise his forehand on stiffened forelegs, so for a couple of seconds he looks like a dog sitting, then uses the muscles of his back and hindquarters to lurch himself up into a standing position. This can take about three seconds in a pain-free, normally strong horse.

Why might he not lie down?

A herd of feral horses never lie down all at the same time. Some will lie out flat to sleep deeply, some will doze and sleep lightly lying down on their breastbone, and others will doze standing up. Yet still others will be awake, grazing and keeping watch. If danger arrives, most of the herd can be fully awake and galloping away within seconds, although those lying out flat will take a few crucial seconds longer.

It is not uncommon for domestic horses in stables too small for them to not lie down, but if a horse in the field refuses to lie down, there is some other problem.

Although horses love rolling in mud and watery patches, they do not like lying down to rest in them. In wet weather on earth enclosures, they rarely lie down, and if they are kept there they may never get any effective rest and sleep.

A horse is likely to refuse to lie down if he is turned out with a horse with whom he does not get along, as he will feel vulnerable in his presence and prefer to remain standing, ready for a quick getaway if necessary.

A common reason for horses not lying down is physical discomfort and pain. Horses with any kind of painful injury, such as a muscle or other soft-tissue tear, will find getting up and down too painful. Weakness, as in debilitated horses, is another reason, as the crucial final action of getting the hindquarters up is too demanding. The average riding horse weighs about 1,000 lbs., so managing his own body is quite a job.

Older horses or those who have led very athletic lives often end up with some form of arthritis later in life. Arthritis is progressive and can be relieved by medication and specific nutrition, but as yet cannot be cured. An arthritic horse (see pages 60–61) will learn that getting down is dangerous because getting up again is more or less impossible.

What to do

- Turn out horses with compatible companions so that they feel secure.
- Keep a close eye on all the horses and make sure you regularly see them getting down and then up again, to roll or sleep.
- If during regular observation you find that a horse does not lie down, check his companions' behavior toward him and, if that is fine, consult your vet.
- Always make sure your horse has somewhere comfortable (soft and dry) to lie down for adequate rest and sleep.

Curiosity and visitors

When content and healthy, most horses have a natural curiosity and like investigating visitors, both human and animal. However, moods can change in a second, so caution is advised.

Above: *Although moving away from something behind them, these horses are curious enough about the photographer to give him their attention.*

What form does it take?

Horses use their senses to inform them of people or animals entering their territory. They may see or hear a visitor first, then when they are close enough will smell, touch, and even try to taste them.

Among horses in a field, curiosity can result in much excitement and flying around, snorting with tails held high and a prancing gait. Anything unusual (to those particular horses), especially if it is near or actually in the field, can cause this reaction. A person carrying an umbrella or pushing a stroller often seems to set them off, as can an unfamiliar animal such as a badger or fox entering the field, if the horses are not used to them. High-sided and pale or brightly colored vehicles can also trigger this reaction.

Often, though, the horses are quieter. They may approach people, other horses, dogs, and wild animals visiting their fields, quietly and calmly. Their ears will be forward, listening for clues as to the visitor's type and identity, their eyes will be focused straight on them, and their nostrils will be flared to catch their scent.

Safety issues

With human visitors on the other side of the fence, horses in a field often approach with ears pricked and an interested look on their faces. They may simply be curious or be looking for food, which unwary humans often carry in their pockets to feed the horses. Feeding the ducks is a good deal safer.

Horses squabbling for tidbits over a fence, particularly barbed wire (which should never be used for horses, as it is too dangerous), can easily get their legs caught in it, breaking a rail as they try to get free or even injuring their legs. A strand of plain wire can become caught between the shoe and heel of a pawing hoof, or a hoof can become trapped in the wire squares of sheep netting (another unsuitable fencing material for horses).

If the visitors enter the field, they can easily be mobbed by horses looking for tidbits.

What to do

If you find yourself the center of attention that is escalating in its intensity, assume a very confident, military-leader type of posture. Draw yourself up and speak firmly and loudly to the horses while looking for an escape route. Often, a change in attitude on your part—from friendly visitor to bossy human—results in the horses backing off and leaving you alone.

Although your visit may start by precipitating friendly curiosity, things can quickly change if jealousy comes into the picture. It is a good idea to always take a rope or stick with you when you enter a field of horses, so that you can swing it

toward them if necessary to get them to back off. Failing this, waving your arms around and shouting, and perhaps walking purposefully or even running toward the horses, should have the desired effect.

Because horses are so curious and inquisitive, it is important to their welfare that they receive enough mental stimulation in their daily lives. Many horses are stabled all day while their owners are at work, and some receive only restricted exercise. If this is unavoidable, consider moving to a yard that will allow your horse daily turnouts with friends. Horse toys are available, and branches in the stable for the horse to chew are usually welcome.

Above: A lonely horse will be pleased to see a visitor, even if she is not his owner.

Feeding in the field

Although fields usually present grass everywhere, sometimes there is not enough good grass to go around and extra feeding becomes necessary. Even with this, there is a right and a wrong way to do it.

What and how to feed

Horses need fiber—and lots of it—including grass, maybe some leaves and roots, and hay or haylage. When grass becomes overgrazed, too short or long, tough and not so sweet, horses can become hungry, fractious, and thin, and also very cold if it is winter.

The most important feed is good hay or haylage, and this will normally be fed in hay nets tied inside a shelter, to fence posts or trees, or in cattle racks. Feeding hay on the ground is wasteful, as much will be trampled underfoot and consequently rejected.

If there is a man-made overhead shelter, short-chopped forage feeds (made from chopped grasses, straw, and alfalfa/lucerne) may be fed in large tubs or troughs inside the shelter, to keep them from getting soaked outside. It is safest to fix the tubs to the walls in corners to stop horses from playing with them, wasting the contents and maybe causing accidents.

If concentrate feeds (grains, pellets, coarse mixes) are provided, this will usually be in individual buckets or tubs. However, among friendly horses that require similar amounts and types of feed, they can be fed in a long trough in a barn or shelter, for communal access.

Right: Large containers, well spaced out like these ones, are good for outdoor feeding, but need to be moved frequently so that the ground does not get poached.

Below: Feeding hay on the ground is wasteful, as horses trample it around and spoil it and then refuse to eat it.

Possible problems

Even friendly horses can become enemies at feed time. If you are at all late, the horses will congregate around the gate, treading it into a quagmire in winter and growing argumentative. This can make entering the field and distributing the feed a risky undertaking.

Once fed, the horses may then play the equine equivalent of musical chairs, swapping from bucket to bucket or hay net to hay net because they seem to think that everyone has better feed than they do. There could be an element of one-upmanship involved, although it is noticeable that the most superior horses are not hassled for their food. This can result in some horses not getting their full ration.

What to do

- Don't keep the horses waiting; feed on time without fail, because they have an internal clock. Disgruntled horses start confrontations and injuries can result.
- Always take more than enough hay (or whatever you are feeding) to last until your next visit. In this way, the horses will not get so hungry that they become miserable and stressed, prone to fighting, and difficult to control when you arrive.

- Feed under cover and on dry standing whenever possible. If you have a field shelter (a necessity for decent accommodation in most domestic fields), fit long hayracks down the walls at the horses' head height, to take the hay. This will keep it dry and palatable, and will avoid wastage.
- If you do not have a shelter, feed in the driest, most sheltered spot and change the exact location every time to prevent the horses from poaching the ground. Always provide at least one more hay net than there are horses to ensure ample opportunity for all to eat.
- When giving bucket feeds, stay to see fair play and take the buckets away with you. You may need a helper for this. If necessary, any horses expected to give trouble can be fed on the end of a lead rope or taken out of the field while feeding.
- If any horse is being bullied for his bucket feed, take him out of the field and feed him separately.

Although it is an extra job, field and shelter feed containers need to be kept reasonably clean. Dried-on food soon accumulates bacteria and smells unpleasant, which puts off many horses (and plastic retains smells), and will gather rainwater and slime. Check them daily, scrub them, and rinse them with clean water. At the same time, check the field water supply.

Is there a herd boss?

Of all the differing opinions in the horse world, this must be the one that is currently most in dispute. Many scientifically trained behavioral therapists and researchers swear that there is no rank order, but others of the same ilk swear there is. Lay horse people usually claim that scientists take too narrow a view, and most of them believe that there most certainly is a herd hierarchy. Can the horses tell us?

HERD COMPOSITION

A feral herd will consist of a family nucleus of mature mares, usually related, and their foals, yearlings, and some older siblings. There is normally one breeding stallion that may hold tenure for a few years, as long as he is physically strong enough to retain his harem and fight off rival stallions. The number of horses in a herd will probably be about a dozen, or maybe fewer. Stallions seem to know how big a herd they can maintain according to existing resources.

Many experts seem to believe that there is not a strict hierarchy or kicking order in a herd, or even an overall herd leader, although elders are normally looked to by younger animals because of their experience. It seems that stallions round up the others more to keep possession of their genetic offspring than to order them around or even protect them.

EFFECTS OF DOMESTICITY

Domesticity can change horses' behavior to some extent, because domestic horses are kept artificially with more physical and psychological pressures on them than feral ones, especially populations that change much more frequently. Horses living in such conditions, such as the average

EVASIONS AND COMPLEXES

Until recently, the word "evasion" featured regularly in the vocabulary of horse people and implied that the horse was being naughty, simply refusing to work willingly. However, things are starting to change as an improved understanding of equine behavior and psychology is generated by the scientific community and filters through to the lay horse world.

A complex is a strong and confirmed dislike or fear of something, seemingly with no apparent reason for it. Most horse people, often in despair, have to deal with one of these at some point. It can be frustrating for us and upsetting for the horse. The problems covered in this chapter are those most commonly encountered and those that seem to cause the greatest concern to both horses and their riders.

Refusing to be groomed

Horses do not care about looking clean and tidy, but most owners spend time every day grooming their horses, and the more a horse refuses to cooperate, the worse the problem becomes. The process should actually be an exercise in gradually establishing trust between you and your horse. Imagine how you would want to be groomed, and behave accordingly.

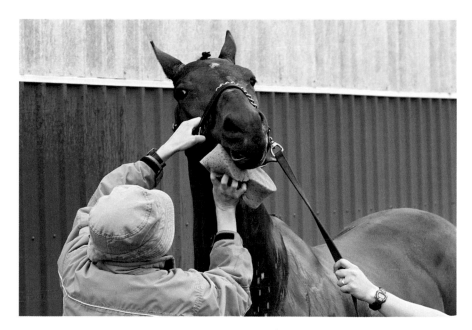

Left: Horses who do not like being sponged liberally with water can still be cleaned with a sponge that is just merely damp.

Far left: Having manes pulled (trimmed) the traditional way is uncomfortable. Use a modern humane trimmer instead.

What is it?

Some horses will allow grooming of certain parts of their bodies, but will object when other parts are reached. Parts that horses often resent being touched are around the head and between the hind legs, and some can become quite violent about it, rearing in hand, pulling back when tied, kicking out, and perhaps even turning to bite.

Possible triggers

Some people are really rough and hurried when they groom their horse. Many horses rightly object to being scrubbed hard, particularly with a dandy brush, which can be excellent when used correctly.

Sometimes, if a horse has had a skin problem or injury on a particular part of his body that has caused him pain or discomfort, he remembers the pain, and although it has long since disappeared, he associates being touched there with distress. This is a shame for the horse, as grooming should be pleasurable and make the horse feel better, as is the case with mutual grooming between horses.

What to do

First, if possible, get someone to hold your horse rather than tying him up. Your helper should give your horse tidbits when he accepts careful grooming from you but not when he objects. Often, it helps to let the horse move around a little or even, in the early stages of his rehabilitation, walk about a bit as you work. This lets him feel less restricted and worried.

You need to use soft brushes and your hands or a soft cloth for a while, even though they are not very effective for cleaning, and gentle, reassuring pressure, but not a tickly touch, which can be irritating.

Glove on a stick

A helpful device that many behavioral therapists use is a stuffed glove fixed on the end of a stick about three feet long. This acts as an extension of the handler's hand and arm to teach the horse to accept reasonable contact, but not to groom him with. It keeps the handler safe and allows them not to back off if the horse objects to contact. For safety's sake, you should ask a professional therapist to use this remedy on your horse rather than trying it yourself.

The therapist quietly strokes the horse nearer and nearer the problem area with the glove. When the horse objects, they keep the glove still without taking it away. When he stops objecting, they take the glove off him as his reward. Some therapists immediately give a tidbit when the horse accepts contact. In this way, the horse associates the glove with reward and objects less to contact.

NATURAL SENSITIVITY

It is important to accept your horse's natural sensitivity in areas like the head and groin, and handle these areas with tact. The head contains all the horse's sensory organs and carries the very sensitive vibrissae, or "feeler hairs," around the eyes and muzzle. The groin is thin-skinned and hairless and contains sensitive structures like the udder, sheath and penis, and testicles. Under the tail is another sensitive area that needs to be handled with care.

Won't go through water

This is a familiar, inconvenient problem for many riders. Because of it, many people have had to retrace their route when only a short distance from home, thereby doubling the length of their ride!

What is it?

The horse is determined to avoid going through any water at all, although he doesn't mind walking on wet surfaces, such as when it is raining.

Where he can, as with a puddle, the horse will walk around the water if the rider does not stop him. Even if the rider tries to direct the horse through it, he will snake his neck and body to avoid the aids, or perhaps even jump the puddle.

When streams, ditches, or rivers are involved, it can be impossible to get a horse over, particularly if the rider starts whipping him, confirming to the horse that the whole scenario is frightening and painful and to be avoided at any cost.

Possible triggers

Horses' feet and legs are precious to them. When we ask them to walk through puddles and streams, or to jump into lakes, they cannot see where they are putting their feet, so this fear is quite reasonable.

Some people think that their horses simply don't like getting their feet wet, and there may well be something to this, as horses often don't like having their legs hosed, either.

If you have a horse that has previously been whipped for not going through water, he will associate it not only with fear but also with pain, so your problems are compounded.

What to do

Horses with this problem need a calm, competent, firm, and positive rider who can be guaranteed not to panic, lose their patience or temper, hit the horse, start shouting, or do anything else that will raise the stakes and make the horse more determined than ever not to go for a paddle. If the horse is frightened, which is quite possible, all this will simply make him worse.

With a young horse, always ride him with others that are guaranteed to go through water and start with something very shallow, even just a pool produced by running the hose on the yard, then fill a dip in the ground with water and take the horses through that. Have experienced horses both in front and behind your horse, and preferably to the sides as well. Use the horse's herd instinct to accompany his leaders through the water, but avoid any kind of force, even a tap with the whip. The experienced company will do the trick sooner or later. The instant the young horse goes through, praise him.

With a confirmed older horse, try the same technique. Start with little more than wet ground and progress gradually, with compliant company, to puddles, shallow fords, or streams with an easy approach. Overfacing the horse, particularly with a difficult approach, is bound to confirm his tendency to refuse. It is always best not to start a battle you can't win. Tact and diplomacy are invaluable.

Try to get him to stand for a few seconds in the water while you feed him tidbits from the saddle, then walk on calmly. As you progress, get the other horses to move farther away from him, and also gradually get your horse to take the lead. This way, you are likely to see success before too long.

Far left: Getting horses used to water is much easier in the company of others who already enjoy it.

Below: If your horse refuses an approach to cross a stream, walk him slowly down and nearer to the water, rather than trying to force him across.

Can't catch him!

This is another quite common problem that can become a habit. It is completely exasperating to be faced with this every day, but how do you get around it?

What is it?

Horses recognize the people who come to bring them in and the things they carry, such as head collars and buckets. If another owner or helper arrives in the field, the horse probably continues grazing, but when someone who normally brings him in arrives, he starts moving away, just far enough to avoid capture, although he will turn it into a merry dance if the person starts running after him. This is obviously useless, as horses can run much faster than people.

Possible triggers

Quite clearly, the horse does not want to come in, sometimes even if he is the only one left in the field. This is because he associates it with being taken away from grass and, quite likely, having to work. If a horse experiences anything unpleasant during work, such as pain, discomfort, confusion, or boredom, he may understandably want to avoid it because of its associations.

It is noticeable that, when the weather and other conditions make being in the field extremely uncomfortable—like driving wind, relentless rain, bitter cold, searing heat, torturing insects, or being bullied—the same horse will be standing by the gate with or without the others, begging to be brought in. He knows where it is most comfortable: in the field with grass and away from work, or in his stable if conditions outside are unbearable.

What to do

Always leave a well-fitting, field-safe (easily breakable) head collar on your horse with a length of twine about six inches longhanging from it.

Left: This is a depressingly familiar picture to any owner of a horse who is hard to catch.

Right: Begging doesn't usually work with horses; this posture in the human is actually psychologically pushing the unwilling horse away from her!

Do not always go to the field to catch your horse. Go sometimes, carrying a head collar or bridle and an empty bucket if these trigger him off, and walk around ignoring him. Then go away. Progress to paying him some attention before leaving, then to leading him a short way, giving him a tidbit, and turning him loose. Then take him through the gate, treat him, and turn him out again. Over time, this works with many horses.

Figure out which food or treat your horse finds irresistible and adopt a distinctive posture, such as hands crossed in front of you, when holding it. Stand in this posture, and as your horse comes toward you, walk backward a little before treating him. Pretty soon, when he sees you standing like that, he will come straight over and let you catch him.

A method that initially is rather time-consuming but which works in the long run is to organize a relay of people (if necessary) and take it in turns to walk after your horse in the field in a nonthreatening way, continually preventing him from grazing and giving him no peace. This seems akin to the "sending away" method some trainers use in a round pen and is not necessarily stress-free for the horse, but it is generally effective, and sooner or later the horse will give up and either come to you or allow you to approach him.

Refusing to be tied up

This is a real nuisance, and also dangerous. Horses can exert a pull one and a half times their own weight, and this will snap most equipment or break the horse's neck.

What is it?

Some horses are fine tied up, provided someone stays with them. As soon as such a horse is left alone, he might start pawing or, being worried and restrained, begin pulling back on his head collar with a sustained, forceful pull until something snaps or the tie ring flies out of the wall like a dangerous missile. Some horses pull back even when you are with them.

Possible triggers

Like many animals and people, horses are naturally terrified of being trapped. With domestic horses, often the attentions they receive when tied up only confirm their dislike of the procedure. Horses that are easy to tie up can be ruined by one painful or frightening experience.

When the horse keeps pulling in an effort to get away, the headpiece of the head collar exerts more and more pressure on his poll, which becomes increasingly painful. This reconfirms to him that being tied up is uncomfortable, distressing, painful, and/or terrifying.

What to do

You need to get your horse to associate being tied up with a measure of freedom and with pleasure, which usually means something good to eat.

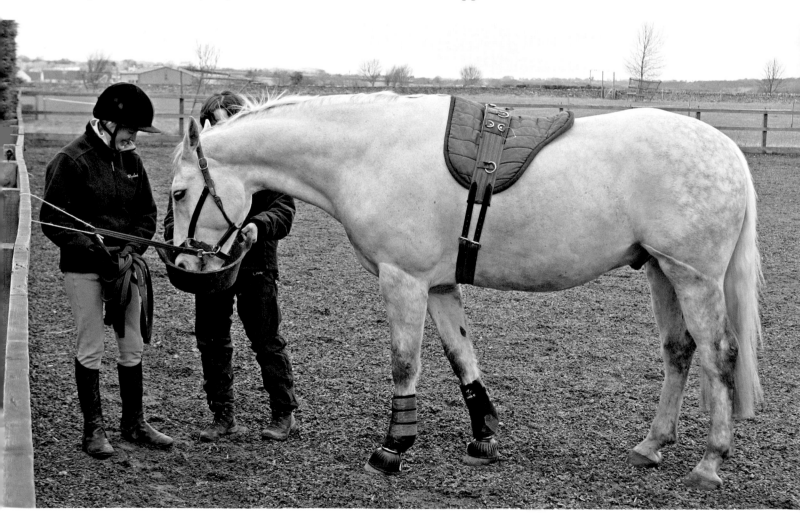

Initially, get someone to hold your horse near a tying-up place, feeding him something he really likes while you deal carefully but confidently with him, perhaps grooming him. Let him move about a little and even let your helper lead him around occasionally, but don't treat him at this time. The handler must not grip the lead rope, exert a sustained pull on it, or hold it close to the horse's head.

Next, get a lunging rein and a roller. Get your helper to give your horse a small, tasty feed while you fasten the rein to his head collar and pass it through a strong string loop on the fence, then back through a side ring on the roller, behind his thighs, and forward through the other side ring.

When your horse has finished eating, during which you have continued to groom him, he will probably start to pull back. In response, pull on the lunging rein, which will cause most horses to move forward again. As soon as he reaches the tying point, your helper should treat him. Over time, he will associate being tied up with nice things: careful attention and, most importantly, food.

Some horses fight the rein behind their thighs and sit down or half-rear. With these, pass the lunging rein from the head collar, through the tie ring (made of twine for safety), and ask your helper to hold it. As you work on your horse, your helper should feed or treat him as long as he is behaving as you wish. If he moves backward, the helper allows the lunging rein to run through the ring or loop and gently draws him back again, treating him when he walks forward. Over time, this technique reassures him that he is not actually tied up, and that being near the tying point involves nice things.

If your horse has had a tying problem, never tie him up without a net of tasty hay, maybe with molasses or peppermint essence on it if he likes these.

It is often advised that you tie up a horse to a breakable string loop on the tying point (see picture opposite) so that if the horse does pull back, the string will break; the horse will get free and will not injure himself or anyone near in his efforts to escape. This is true, but it is also true that once a horse has learned that he can break free he will usually do it regularly. The answer is to train him to get the habit of standing tied, as described here. He must habitually obey "stand" and must learn to associate being tied up with good things.

Left: Giving your horse hay whenever he is tied up gives him plenty of reason to stay put safely.

Far left: These handlers are using the method described above to teach a horse to associate being tied up with good things.

The head-shy horse

This is a common problem and one that can be really inconvenient, especially if you are short and your horse is tall, because the horse can easily keep his head out of your reach.

Left: Horses' heads are sensitive, so they must be handled carefully to avoid any pain or discomfort that may lead to head-shy behavior.

Right: Once a horse is head-shy he will always have a tendency to be that way, but great improvements can be made with patient, correct treatment. A behavioral therapist should also be able to help.

What is it?

A head-shy horse simply does not want his head to be touched. He holds it right up in the air well out of your reach, or waves it around if he is smaller, turning it away from you and trying to back away. This sometimes only happens when the bridle arrives, but some horses also do it when you try to put a head collar on them or groom and clean their heads and faces.

It can be quite galling to see your horse behaving perfectly for someone else when his teeth are attended to. This is often due to nothing more than the confident, calm attitude of the vet or dental technician.

Possible triggers

Horses' heads are one of their most sensitive areas and the smallest association with unpleasant sensations can make a horse become head-shy.

A common reason is that people are rough with the head, maybe without realizing it, and the horse simply does not like it. Someone may have gripped an ear, or even twitched it, to

get him to be still, and this will have been extremely painful and frightening.

With horses that only wave their heads around or put them up in the air when they see the bridle, it is obvious that they associate the bridle and being ridden with unpleasantness, maybe harsh aids, too-hard work, becoming tired out, or being forced to do things they find difficult or impossible.

What to do

The glove-on-a-stick technique (see pages 144–145) often works on a head-shy horse too. It can be used for any area the horse places out of bounds because the handler/therapist can keep up gentle contact while staying out of harm's way should the horse want to leap about or behave defensively.

When treating head-shyness, it is safer to get a competent and sensible helper to hold the horse during the process. If the horse is tied up, he may pull back hard and either lose his footing and fall, break the head collar, and/or learn that he can break away when tied up.

Training your horse to obey the command "head down" will help in mild cases, particularly if he knows you will give him a delicious treat when his head is down but not when he waves it around. Simply stand by his side, bend down, point to the ground, and say "Head down." Many horses will respond to this. If yours doesn't, exert a firm, steady, but not harsh pull downward on the lead rope; the instant the head goes down, release the pressure. This gives him escape from the pressure and he learns to drop his head to relieve himself. A treat always helps if given immediately when he obliges. You can also use the treat to get him to lower his head, accompanying the movement with the command.

Your horse's reactions can be greatly improved over time if you are always careful when handling his head, speaking calmly in a low tone, and giving a treat occasionally during the process. Getting the horse to trust that you will not hurt him, and to associate the process with good things, should result in a considerable improvement in time.

Refusing to load

At every equestrian gathering, you will see a horse refusing to load into his vehicle to go home. You would think that he would want to go home, but apparently not.

What is it?

The horse is led toward the ramp of the vehicle and plants his forefeet at the bottom, or gets partway up and backs down again, falls or jumps off the side, starts circling on the end of his lead rope, or simply won't go anywhere near the ramp.

Possible triggers

Many people believe that troublesome loaders and travelers are claustrophobic, and this may be at least partly true. As a species, horses did not evolve to live in or enter dark, enclosed spaces, particularly those that rattle, rock, lurch, and swing around. The first time a horse is persuaded (usually by following his dam) to enter a vehicle, the inside of it alone may be enough to put him off, even though his dam is standing quietly. He will remember his apprehension even though nothing awful happened to him.

Certainly, an unpleasant journey with a rough, uncaring driver—and with the horse tied up and helpless, lurching around—could be seen as equivalent to mental torture, which sets the future pattern.

A painful incident such as a road accident, a fall inside the vehicle, or being uncomfortable (either too cold or too hot, cramped up, tied short, or traveling with a disliked or feared companion), can cause a firm association of traveling with fear.

Having been forced into a vehicle in the past will also condition a horse to be frightened in the future.

Some horses dislike not being able to see out of their vehicle, whereas others travel better when they actually cannot do so. Obviously, try both ways to discover your horse's preference.

Left: Staring a horse in the face will make a horse even more reluctant.

Below: A confident loader, showing his handler the way. The only improvement would be for the handler to look up into the box.

DRIVING TACTICS

The most important thing for any driver of a horse transport is to imagine that they have no brakes. This will effectively control their speed, acceleration, braking, and turning.

What to do

Because any kind of coercion or removal of options can be seen by the horse as unpleasant or frightening, it is best if at all possible not to transport your horse until his behavior has been greatly improved by means of a long-term and patient retraining process. The horse has to associate the vehicle and traveling with pleasure and, for most horses, this means his favorite food and the presence of a friend. He also has to know that he will not be made uncomfortable or become frightened in the vehicle.

If possible, start by leaving the vehicle in his paddock with the ramp down and delicious food inside, so that he has to enter to get the food and can walk out again forward. Do not attempt this with a trailer that does not have a front unload (unless you have a very small pony), as the horse may try to turn around to get out, and become stuck.

Begin with the food on the bottom of the ramp and gradually move it up until it is right at the front of the vehicle. The horse voluntarily enters and eats the food with pleasure. This simple method has reformed many horses.

If the horse is given all his feeds at home in the vehicle, he will soon load with no trouble. Practice loading him without a subsequent journey, giving him treats throughout when he is good. Don't hesitate to load a good loader first and let yours follow, maybe straight through the box at first, then standing them both for a while and unloading again.

The final stage is to load your horse in the usual way and take him for a short roundtrip home again, well driven and with hay. After this, try to take him somewhere familiar, unload him, and load him up again to come home. After that, he should be no trouble.

Index

Acknowledgments

Executive Editor Trevor Davis
Senior Editor Lisa John
Executive Art Editor Penny Stock
Designer Ginny Zeal
Production Controller Manjit Sihra
Picture Research Emma O'Neill

Author acknowledgments

I would like to thank Horsepix for their painstaking efforts to provide the right photos, and the editorial team at Hamlyn for their conscientious approach and helpful attitude, which makes an author's life so much easier.

The author's Web site address is www.susanmcbane.com.

Photographic acknowledgments

Action Library Bauer Action Library/Matthew Roberts 66
Action Plus Neil Tingle 89
Alamy Juniors Bildarchiv 127, Luca DiCecco 62, Mark J. Barrett 7, 40, 50, Mike Hill 45, Rachel Hotchkiss 110, Sigrid Dauth Stock Photography 33 above, tbkmedia.de 15, the National Trust Photolibrary/David Noton 140 left, Tim Graham 17 below, 112
Ardea 123, Chris Harvey 69
Bob Langrish 2, 8, 10 left & right, 12, 13, 14, 17 above, 22, 23, 26, 27, 29, 31, 33 below, 35, 36, 37, 43, 46, 47, 48, 49, 52, 56, 57, 58, 59, 60 left & right, 63, 65, 72, 73, 74 below, 81, 83, 85 below, 85 above, 100, 102, 113, 114, 115, 118, 119, 124, 125, 126, 128, 130, 131, 132, 134, 135, 136, 140
Christina Handley Photography 54, 145
CLix Photography Shawn Hamilton 19, 39, 87
Corbis 44, Image Source 78
Dreamstime.com Amaxim 133 right, Ellende 129
FLPA Richard Becker 151
Gloria McDonald, Wild Mane Photos 38
Horsepix 4, 21, 24, 28, 34, 51, 53, 55, 61, 64, 68, 75, 76, 77, 79, 80, 82, 88, 90, 92, 94, 95, 96, 99, 101, 103, 105, 106, 109, 111, 116, 117, 137, 139, 142, 148, 149, 150, 153
HorseStock.biz 98
Houghton's Horses 18, 20, 30, 42, 70, 71, 86, 91, 93, 108, 120, 122, 138, 146, 154, 146 left, 155
istockphoto.com 144
Linda Sherrill 152
Lucy Griffiths Photography 107
SuperStock Age-fotostock 104